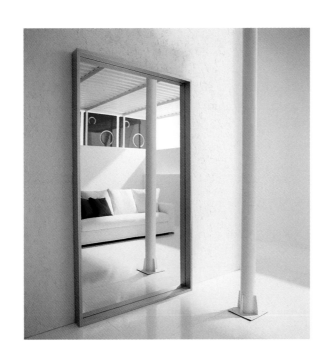

Publishing Director
Nacho Asensio

Editorial coordination and original texts
Patricia Bueno

Design and layout
Núria Sordé Orpinell

English translation
Peter Miller / Simon Thornton

Production
Juanjo Rodríguez Novel

Copyright © 2002 Atrium Group
C/ Ganduxer, 112,1°
08022 Barcelona (Spain)
Tel:+ 34 93 254 00 99
Fax: + 34 93 211 81 39
e-mail: atrium@atriumgroup.org
www.atriumbooks.com

First published in 2002 by HBI, an imprint
of HarperCollins International
10 East 53rd Street. New York, NY 10022-5299

Internationally distributed by HBI, an imprint
of HarperCollins International
10 East 53rd Street. New York, NY 10022-5299
Fax: (212) 207.7654

ISBN: 0-06-053993-3

Editorial Project: Books Factory, S.L.
e-mail: books@booksfactory.org

Dep.Legal: B-37.863-2002

Printed in Spain
ANMAN Gràfiques del Vallès, S.L.

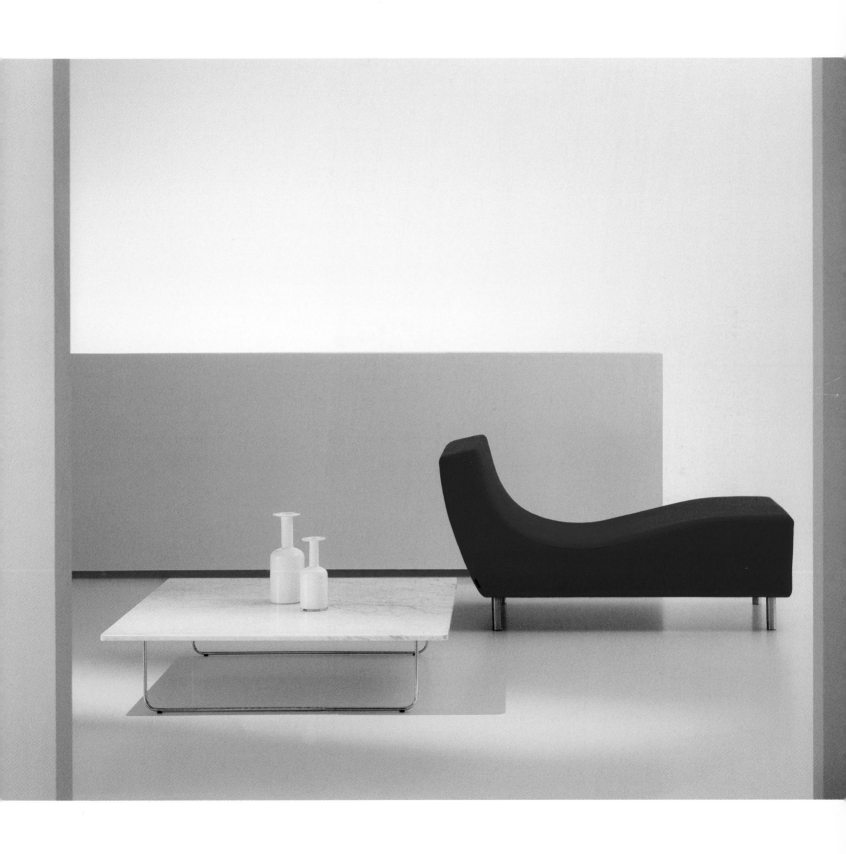

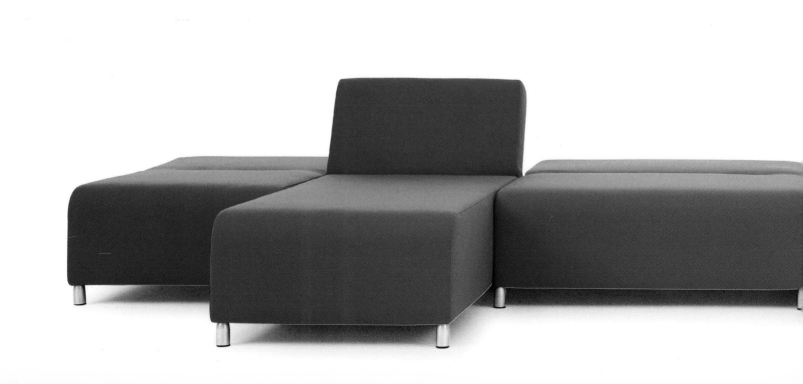

contents

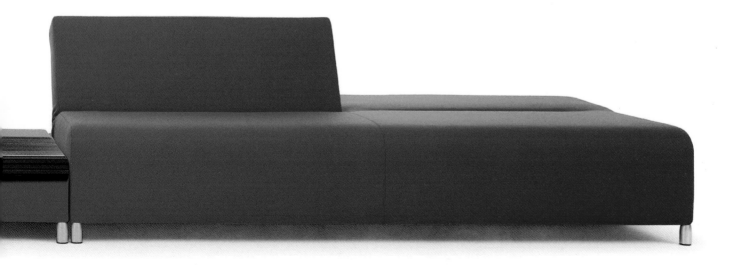

introduction

Minimalism, where interior decoration is concerned, cannot be looked at as a stylistic trend or fashion, but rather something which crosses these frontiers, and becomes an authentic philosophy of life. It seeks the construction of a new society, one anchored only to the essential and which therefore moves away from materialistic eagerness.

Although the means employed are relatively new –minimalism has been exercising its influence on the concept of domestic space for a little more than a decade-, the utopian search for a lifestyle based on simplicity goes back a long way. Its roots are found beyond the theories and geometric shapes of *Bauhaus*, beyond the "less is more" coined by Mies van der Rohe: the rigorous renunciation of the monastic cells from the Middle Ages, the Japanese "wabi-sabi" aesthetic of voluntary poverty, and the spirituality of the Zen philosophy, with its cult of emptiness, are some of the sources of inspiration.

From this perspective, the application of the color in a minimalist environment is no longer a paradoxical or apparently contradictory presence, but rather it becomes a means of expression and contrast, capable of communicating a great deal with a simple brush stroke. On the other hand, this vision also reflects a certain erosion of the strictest minimalism, that which preaches total adhesion to the color white and the elimination of any kind of ornamentation, and its necessary evolution towards more flexible forms, which permit greater freedom of choice of the individual.

Living in a minimalist ambience is an option which implies an effort of renunciation and containment, of liberation from all useless things, of reduction to the basic elements. This means that, to achieve a home where minimalism makes sense, honesty with oneself, the capacity to live with the minimum, must be the first step. Thus, starting out from this strategy of formal reduction, the spatial and material qualities of the house are boosted, creating an atmosphere which has a direct bearing on the sensory experience. Color, therefore, contributes to the enriching of this experience generated in emptiness, granting a specific meaning to this way of life.

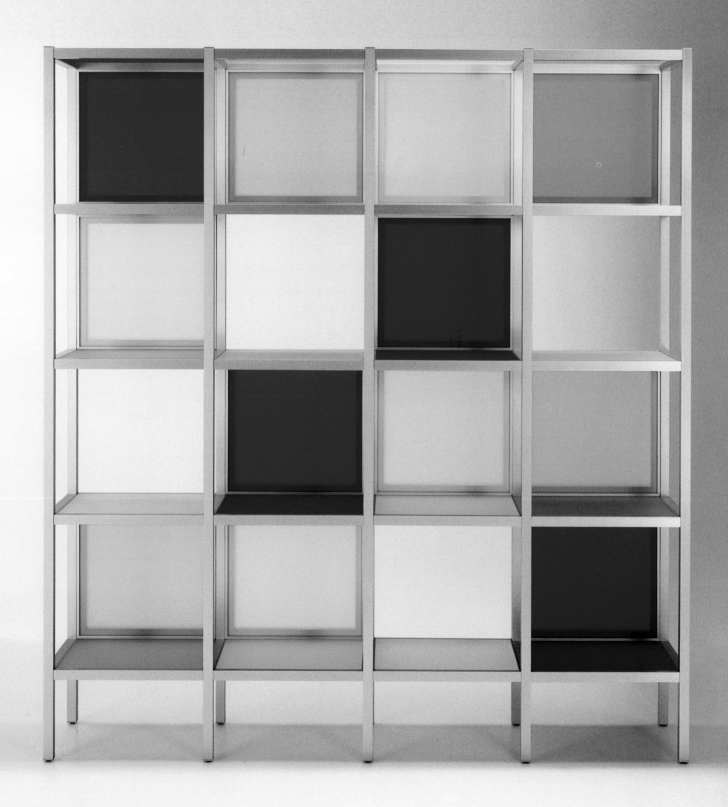

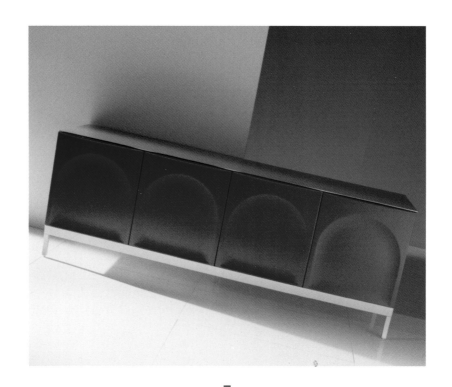

■

"The suppression of decoration is
necessary to regulate passion."

Adolf Loos

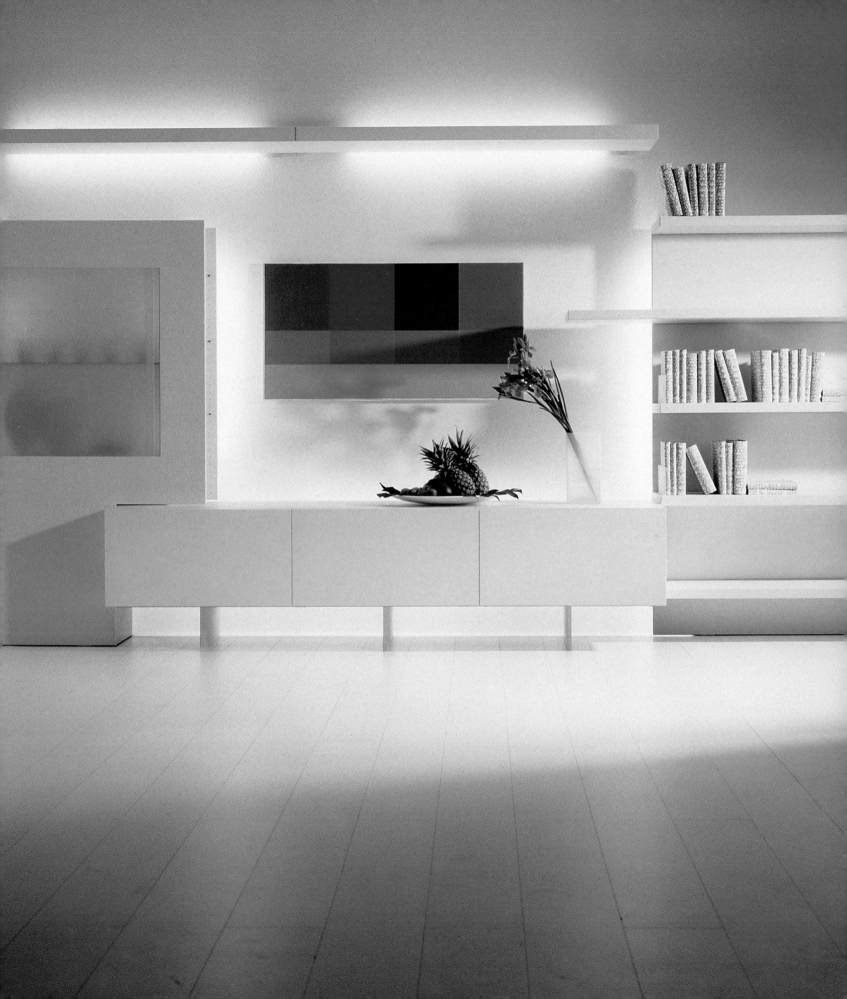

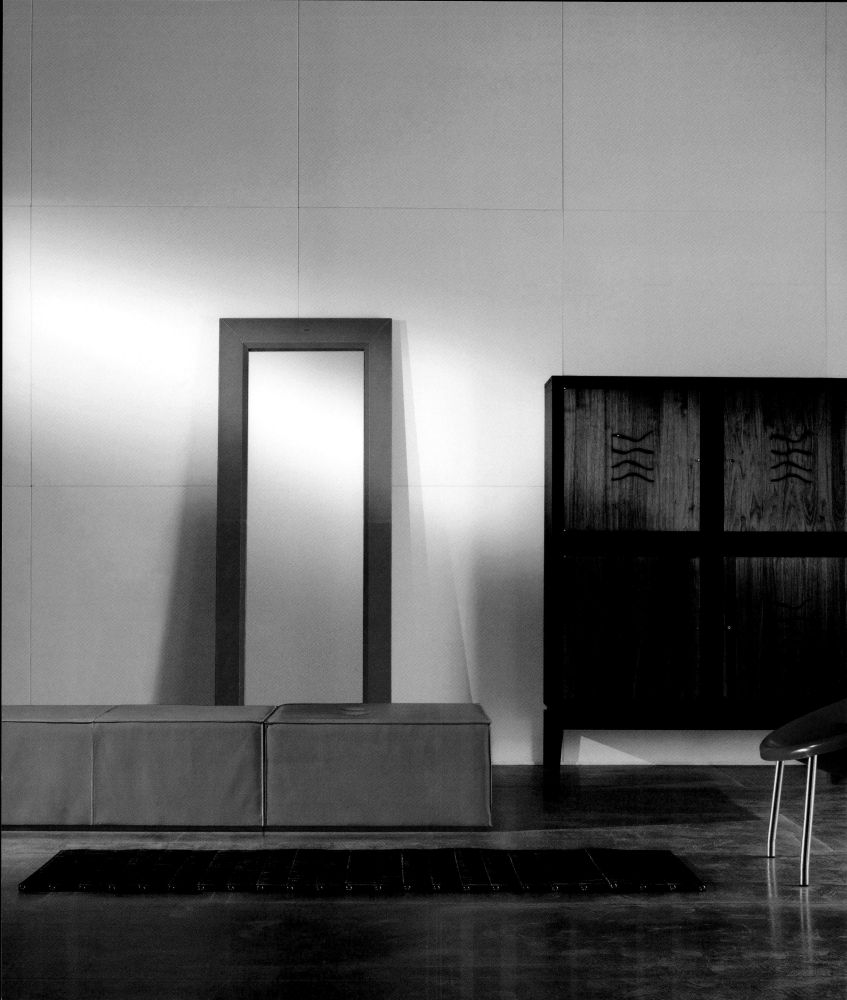

Interiors & Minimalism: Influences

Minimalism & The Modern Movement

In order to precisely define Minimalism, it is necessary to study its origins in the Modern Movement, identified with functionalism, which was developed in Europe after the First World War. It came about as architects, designers and craftsmen, united by a spirit of innovation, reacted against the dominance of Historicism, which had been present in previous styles. The result was a radical change in the cultural and aesthetic sensitivity of society, particularly evident in art and literature.

Of a more ideological than aesthetic nature, the representatives of the Modern Movement, especially those of the *Bauhaus School,* understood design as a means of improving society, from changing the conceptions of building construction to the creation of a simple chair.

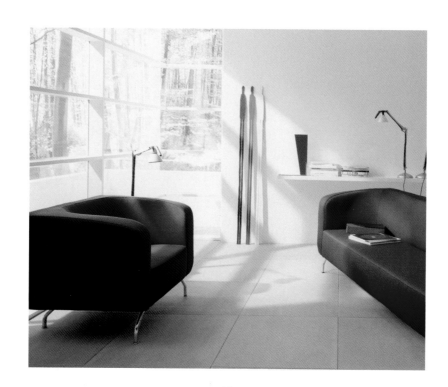

"There are two ways to achieve joy and happiness. One way is to highlight the sensual beauty of everything that surrounds us. The other is to eliminate anything that might cast a shadow over it."

Ou Baholyodhin

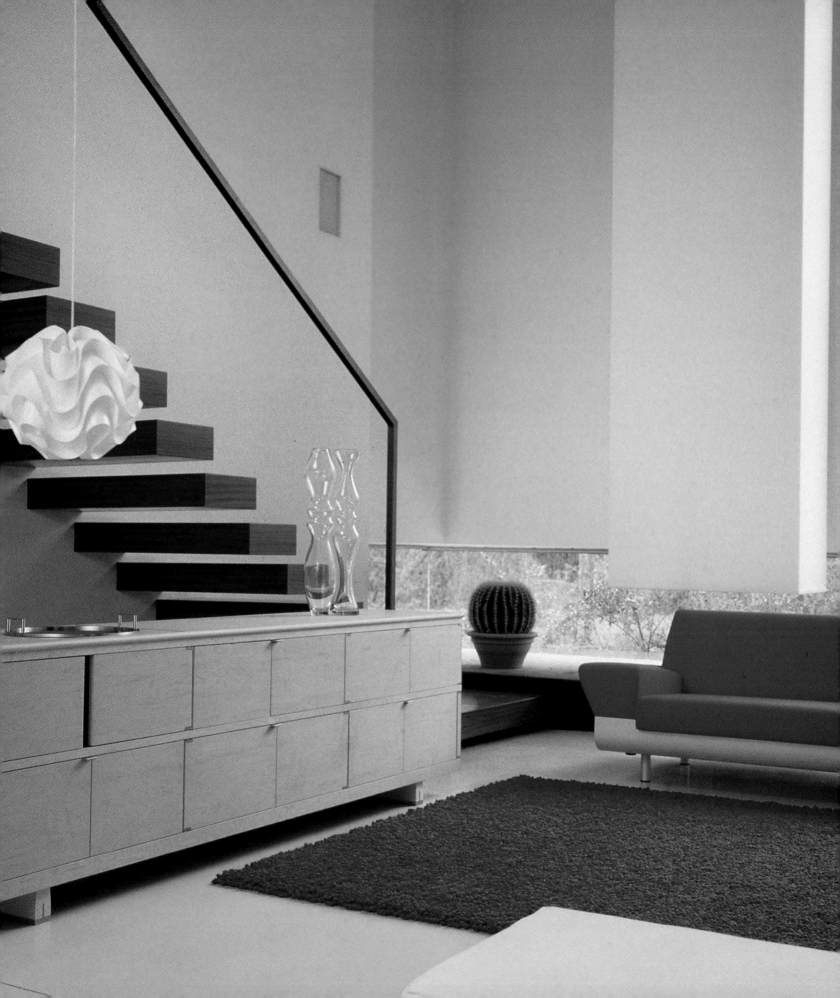

In this sense, one can observe the influence of the Arts and Crafts movement, which developed in the United States and Great Britain between the end of the 19th century and the beginning of the 20th. The objective of introducing social and aesthetic reforms based on the restoration of craftsmanship and on designs based on simple straight forms made from natural materials, gave rise to the creation of furniture that led to the geometric style of the De Stijl group and the *Bauhaus School*, founded by Walter Gropius in 1919. In the United States, the movement focused on a predominant theme: the democratic interest in glorifying the virtues of honesty and simplicity in the design of objects intended for daily use. From this relation arise three key concepts that we find in the basis of modern day minimalist interiors: geometry, simplicity and honesty.

Within minimalist decoration, we can observe shapes that remind us of the De Stijl group, developed between 1917 and 1928, which produced some of the most representative designs of the 20th century, such as the geometric paintings of Piet Mondrian and the revolutionary furniture of Gerrit Rietveld. Its connection with contemporary minimalist style can be observed in the principal formal constants of De Stijl: the use of rectangles and squares in flat planes of bold primary colors, together with black, gray and white, all carefully orchestrated with straight lines.

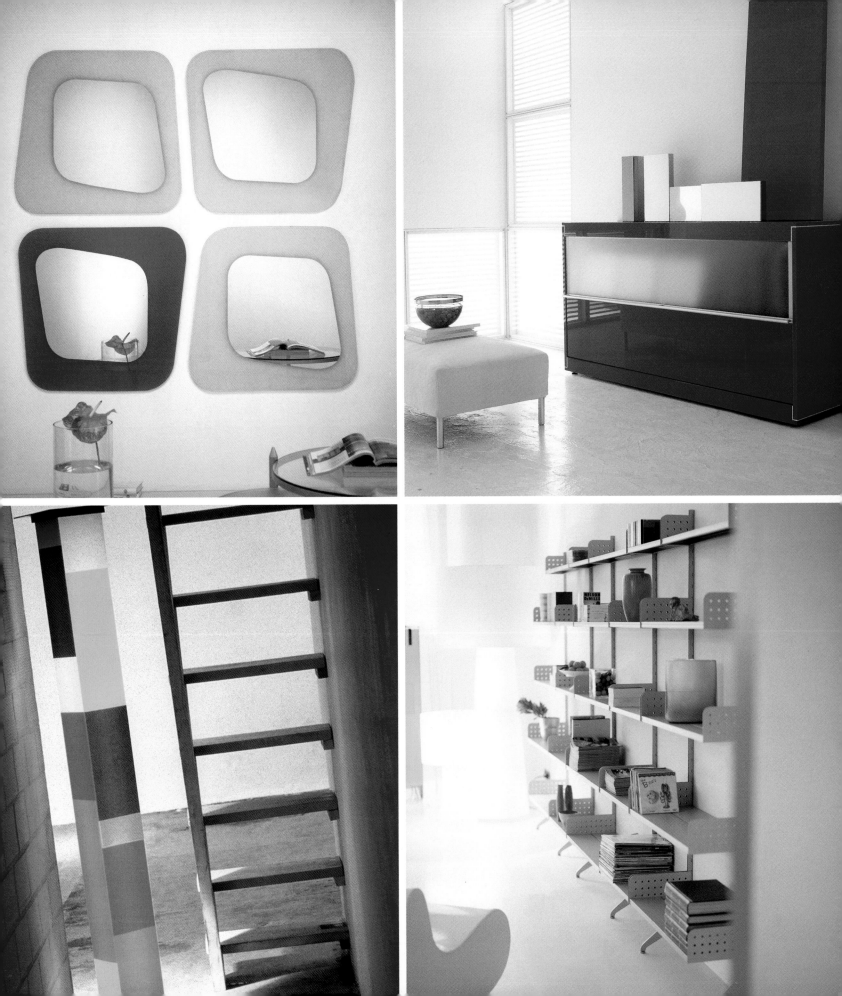

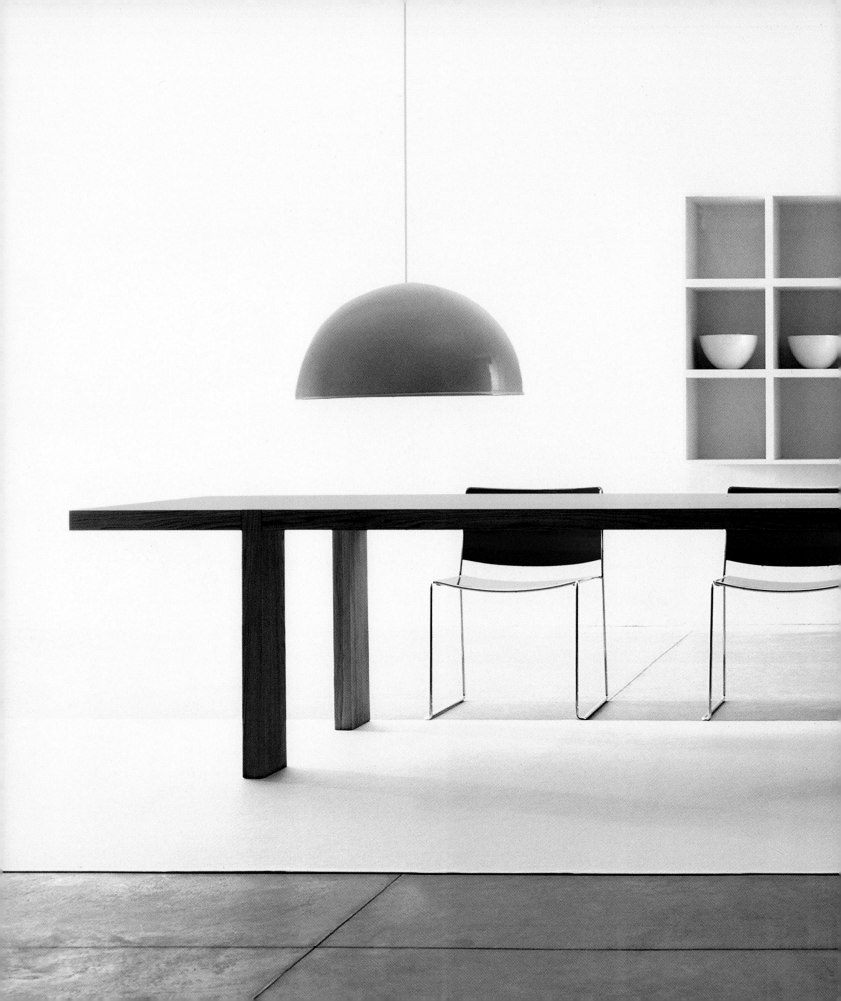

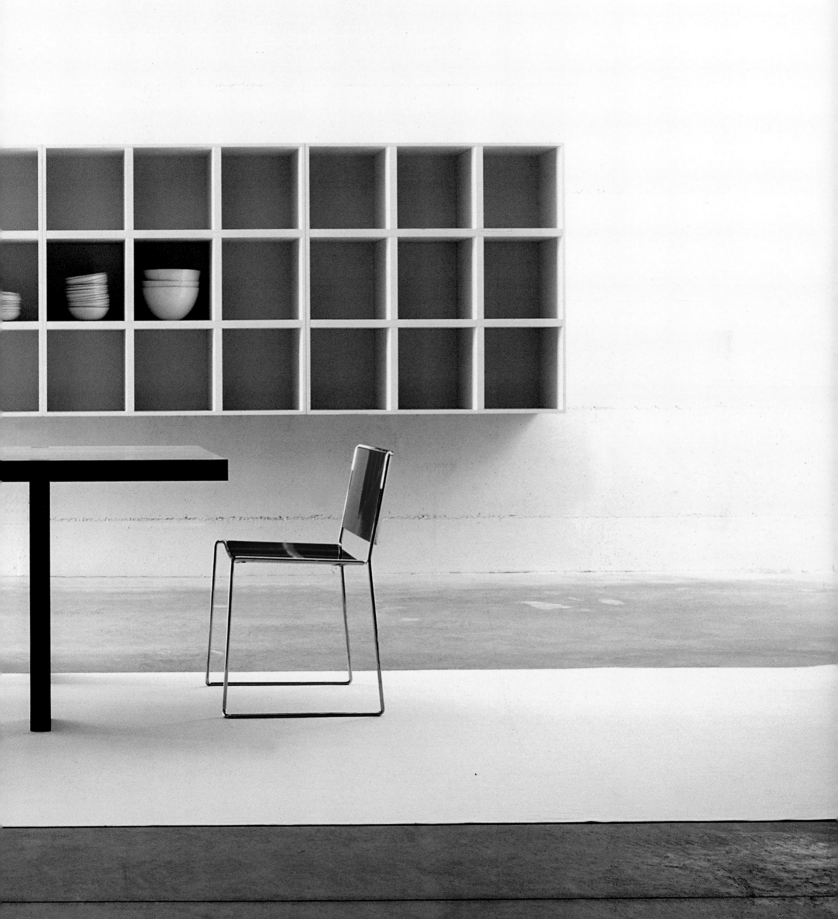

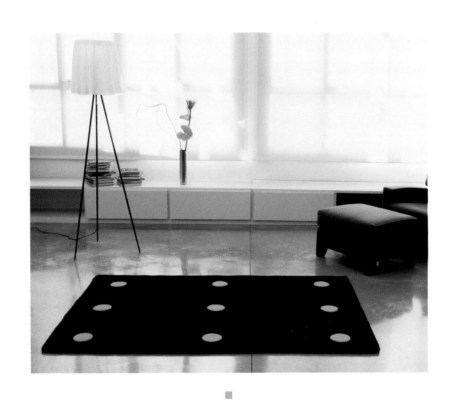

"A place becomes your home when
you are sincere."

Ou Baholyodhin

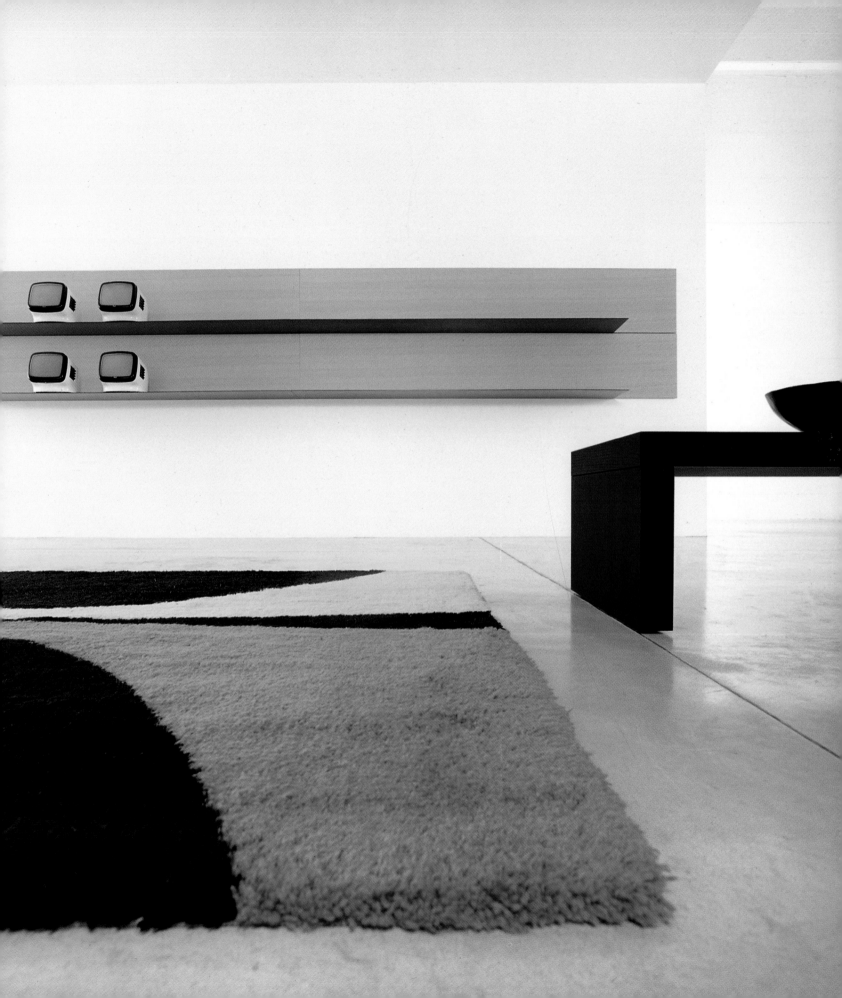

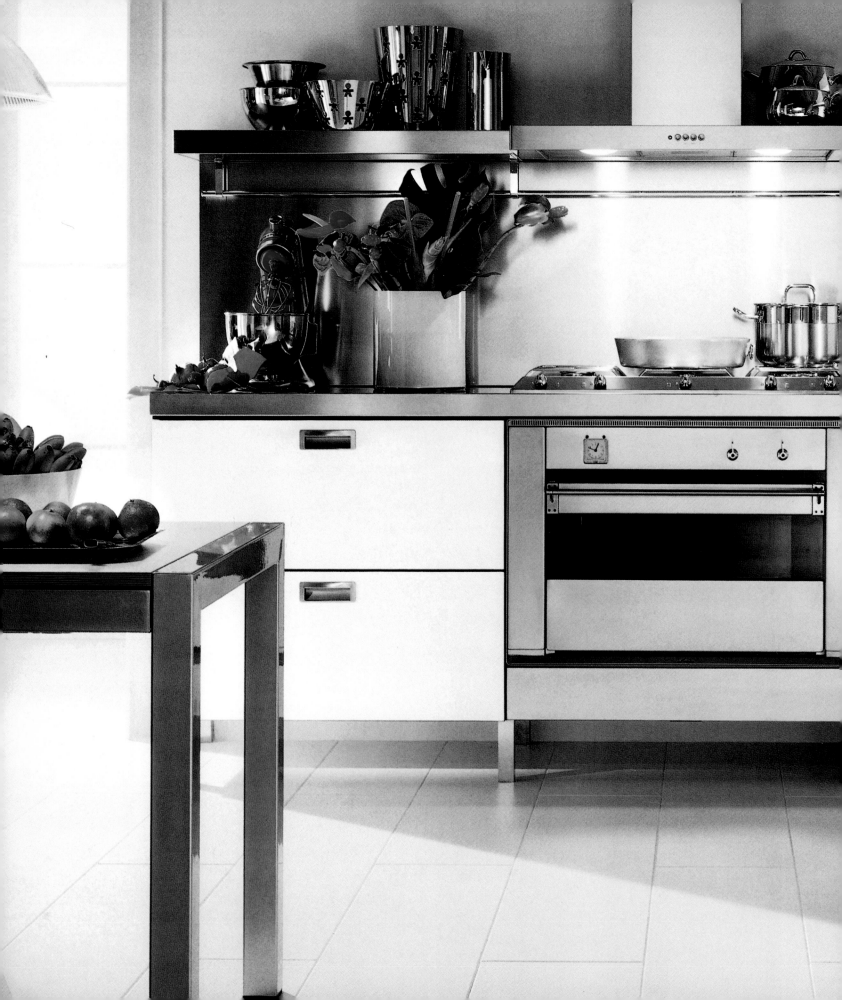

As far as the aesthetic premises established by *Bauhaus* are concerned, apart from the already mentioned concepts of geometry, simplicity and honesty, one can also extract further influences that have been absorbed by minimalism: universality, direct expression, standardization, economy and the application of new technologies. However, the contribution of the *Bauhaus School* with regard to the creation of a new domestic environment does not only take shape today through its influence on minimalism but also through the practical innovations that were introduced, namely the marriage of engineering and craftsmanship. These innovations have profoundly affected current industrial design and have come to form part of our lives. As Frank Whitford comments in his book, *Bauhaus*, "Everyone sitting on a chair with a tubular steel frame, using an adjustable reading lamp, or living in a house partly or entirely constructed from prefabricated elements is benefiting from a revolution in design largely brought about by the *Bauhaus*".

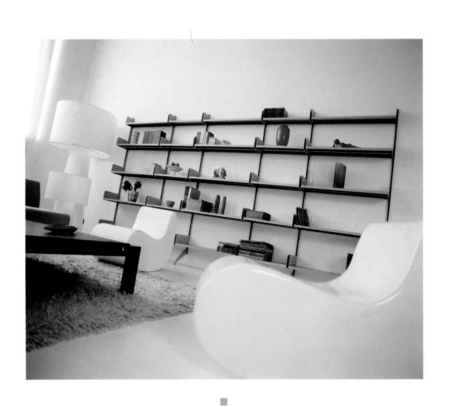

The introduction of color accents within
a world of whiteness recalls the fact
that white light is the origin of the whole
spectrum of colors.

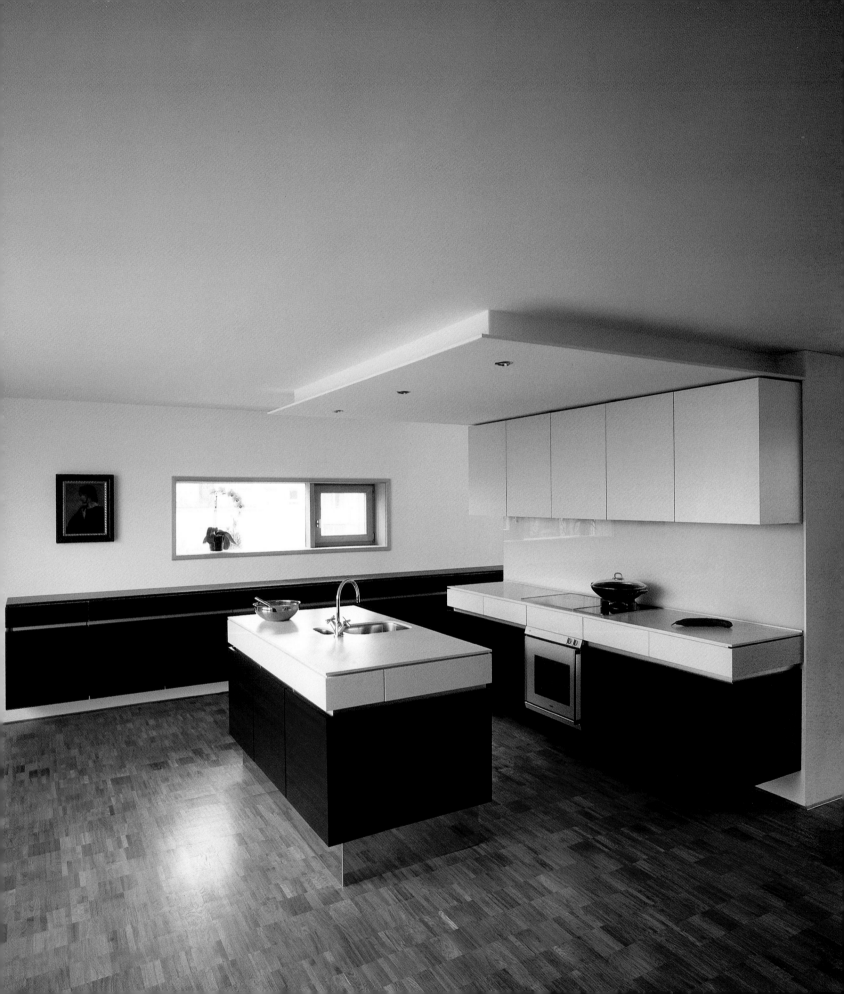

At the base of this revolution can be found one of the principal *Bauhaus* proposals, established by Gropius, "to make modern artists become familiar with science and economy, by uniting creative imagination with a practical knowledge of craftsmanship, and thus to develop a new sense of functional design." This concept took shape through three principal objectives: primarily, to encourage individual craftsmen in different fields to work together and combine their skills; secondarily, to elevate the status of crafts (chairs, lamps, teapots etc.) to the same level enjoyed by fine arts (painting, sculpture etc.) by affirming that a house and the utensils found within have to sensibly relate to each other; tertiarily, to maintain contact with the leaders of industry, in order to sell their work and gain independence from government support.

One of the most prominent representatives of the *Bauhaus School*, its director between 1930 and 1933, Ludwig Mies van der Rohe, is fundamental to the very genesis of minimalism. Considered to be the mòst representative minimalist architect of the 20th century, his notion of universal space turned empty spaces into a cornerstone of his work. In interiors, he proposed molding empty spaces, dilating them until he removed the barriers between interior and exterior. To do this, he freed the interior space of traditional structures and enclosures, like columns and walls, which had always been used to create different rooms. This new conception of space, full of significant emptiness, reminds us of present day lofts, the paradigm of a new lifestyle based on freedom and the search for simple forms.

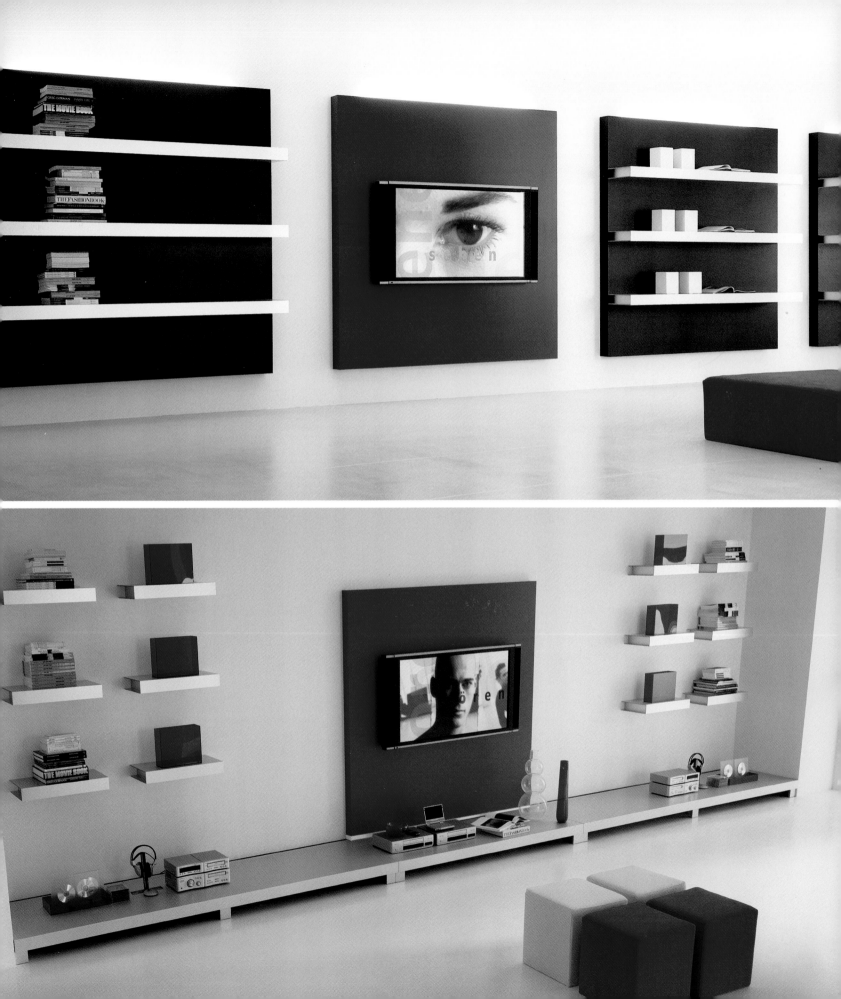

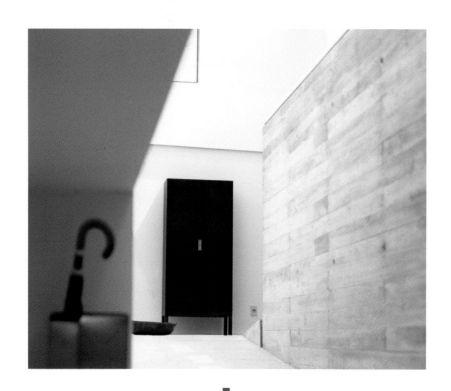

"But, after all, the aim of art is to create
space – space which is not occupied by
decoration or illustration, space within
which the subjects of painting can live."

Frank Stella, minimalist artist

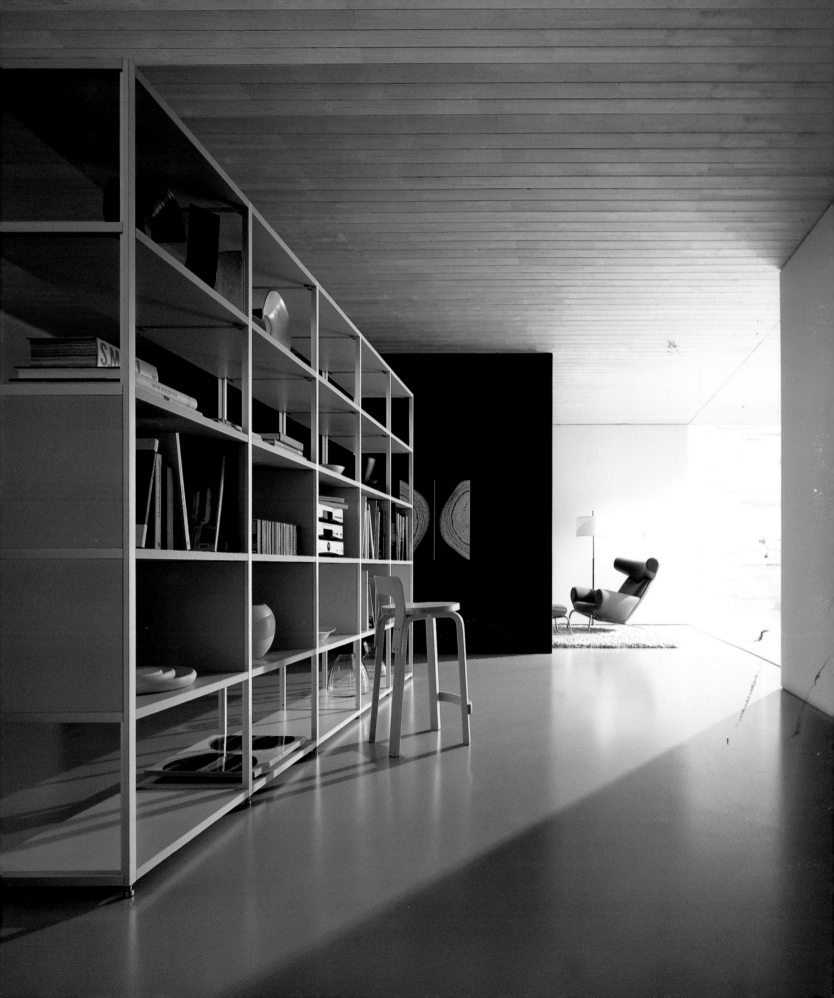

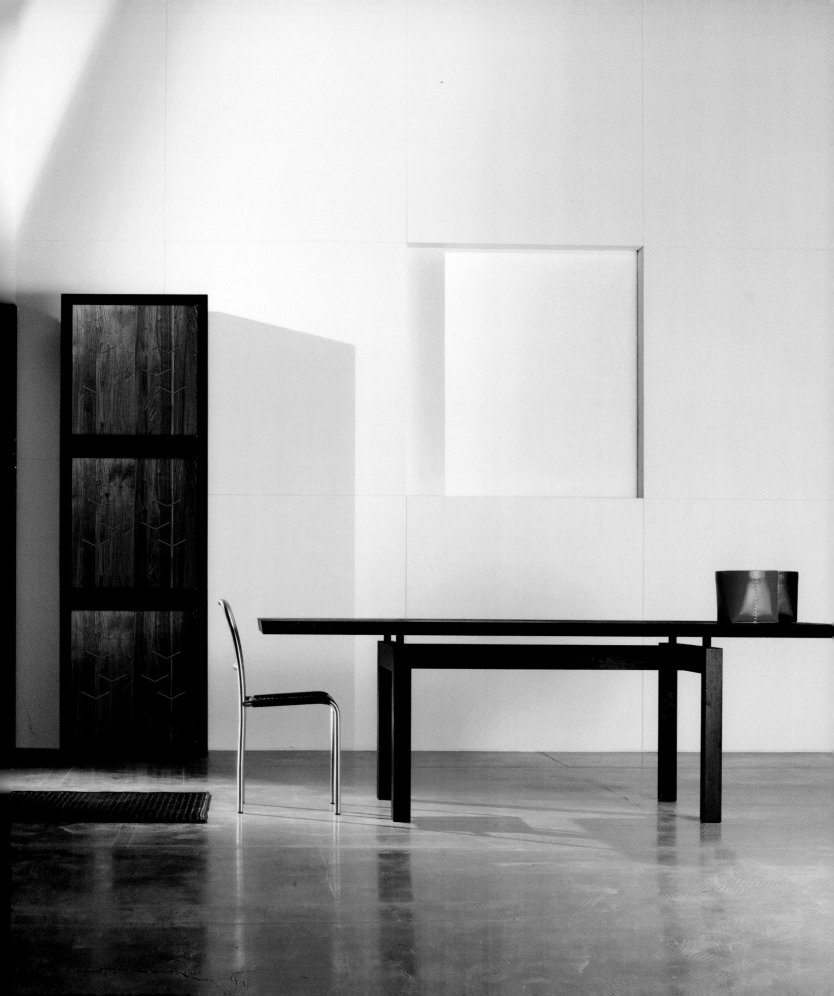

Amongst Mies van der Rohe's work the Barcelona German Pavilion, built in 1929 for the Universal Exhibition and considered by many critics to be the quintessence of spatial abstraction in architecture, is a perfect example to see the parallels between his architecture and today's minimalist interiors. In both cases, the empty space takes on meaning through the direct experience of each person. When visiting the pavilion, or when entering a minimalist home, moving around the space allows the apparent severity and austerity of these spaces to be transformed into an eloquent composition, giving the atmosphere an indescribable spirituality.

In 1933, when the Nazi majority came to power, the *Bauhaus School* was closed and the majority of its leaders, including Gropius and van der Rohe, emigrated to the United States. The American adaptation of *Bauhaus* architecture took on the name of the International Style, developing, along with its technological and ideological contributions, skyscraper architecture, consequently becoming a symbol of capitalism. The premise of this style was the development of an impeccable architecture based on pure geometrical forms. Thus, purity, smooth flat surfaces, and simplicity attained through the removal of ornamentation are some of the concepts associated with these projects, among which we can find the constructions made by Le Corbusier, one of the most influential architects of the 20th century. The Seagram Building in New York, built in bronze and glass and designed by Mies van der Rohe in collaboration with Philip Johnson, is considered to be one of the best-known examples of the style.

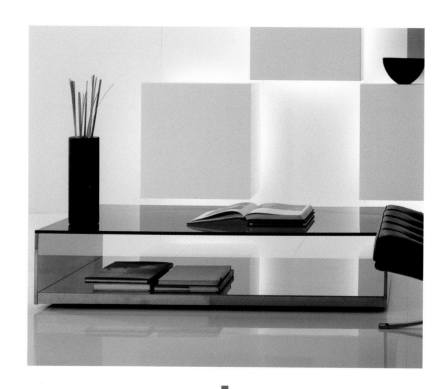

"Each moment eclipses the one before.
Whatever happens, this is the present.
Build your house here."

modern Zen meditation

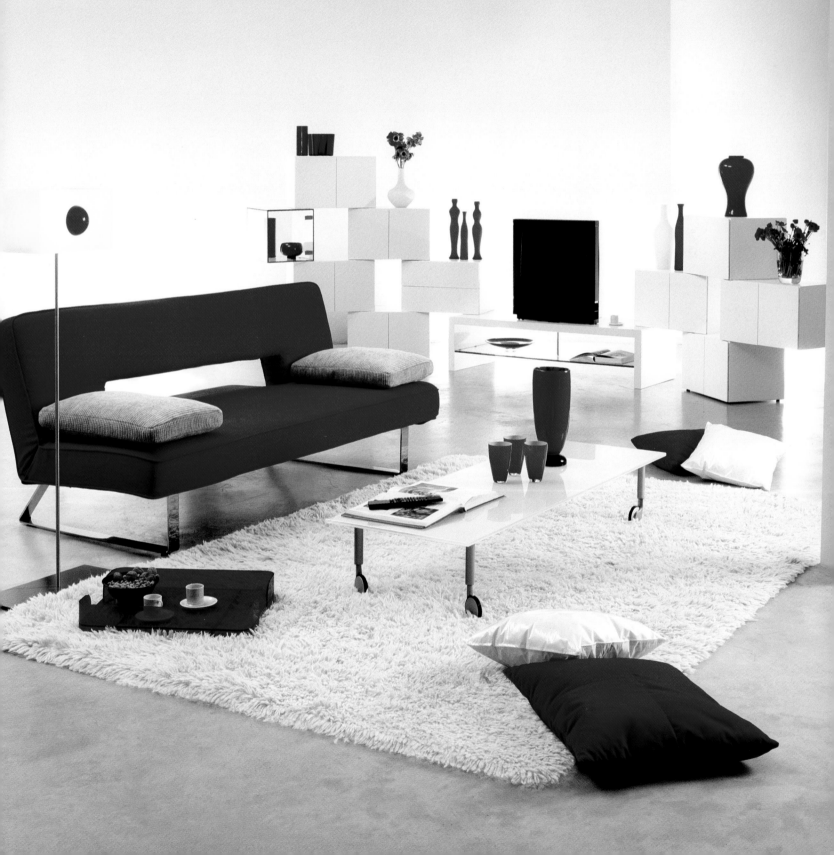

The representatives of this new architecture aimed to create universal structures with a powerful presence that portray lightness, using technology that permits the design of open plans, that increase the entrance of natural light. The majority of contemporary architecture falls within these formal constants.

Minimalism & Art

The term Minimalism was applied for the first time to an artistic movement developed at the end of the 1960s in the United States, as a reaction against the subjectivism of Abstract Expressionism and against the visual greed of the society of that era. For this reason, minimalist works of art are reduced to a minimum number of colors, values, shapes, lines and textures. The exponents of this style proposed a quest for the essential, eliminating from the work of art any evidence whatsoever of the artist's hand and fleeing from the notion of art as a means of personal expression, revealing their rejection of representing or symbolizing any type of object or experience.

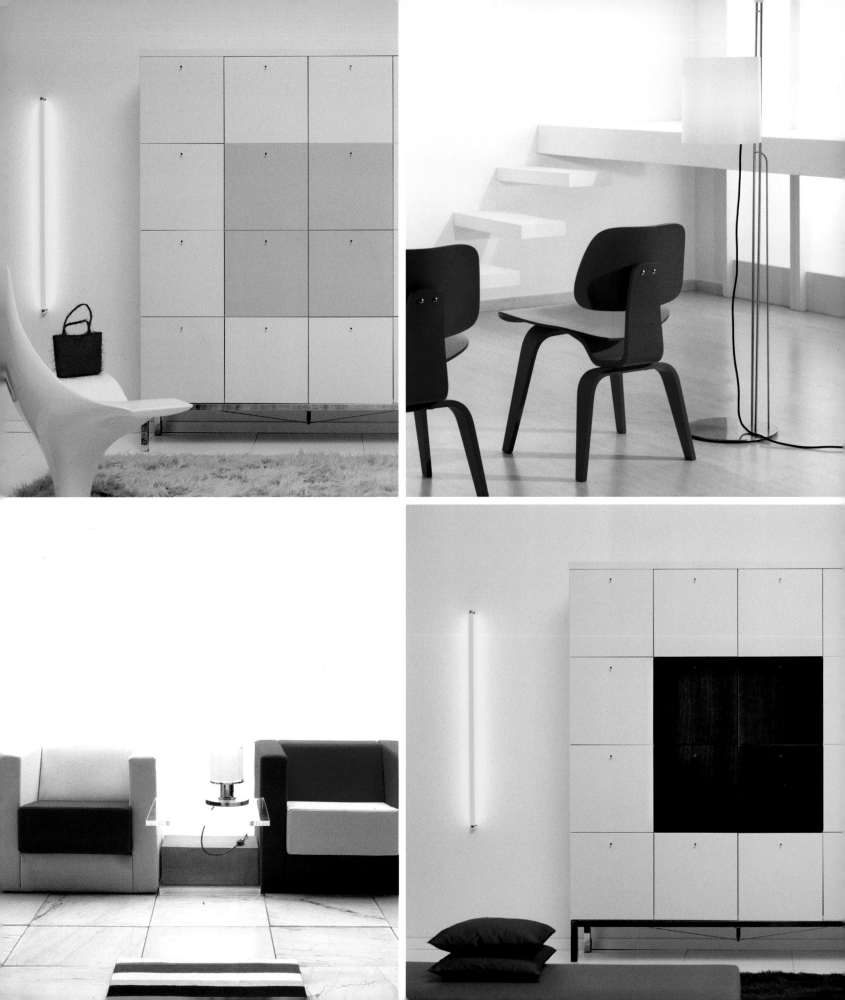

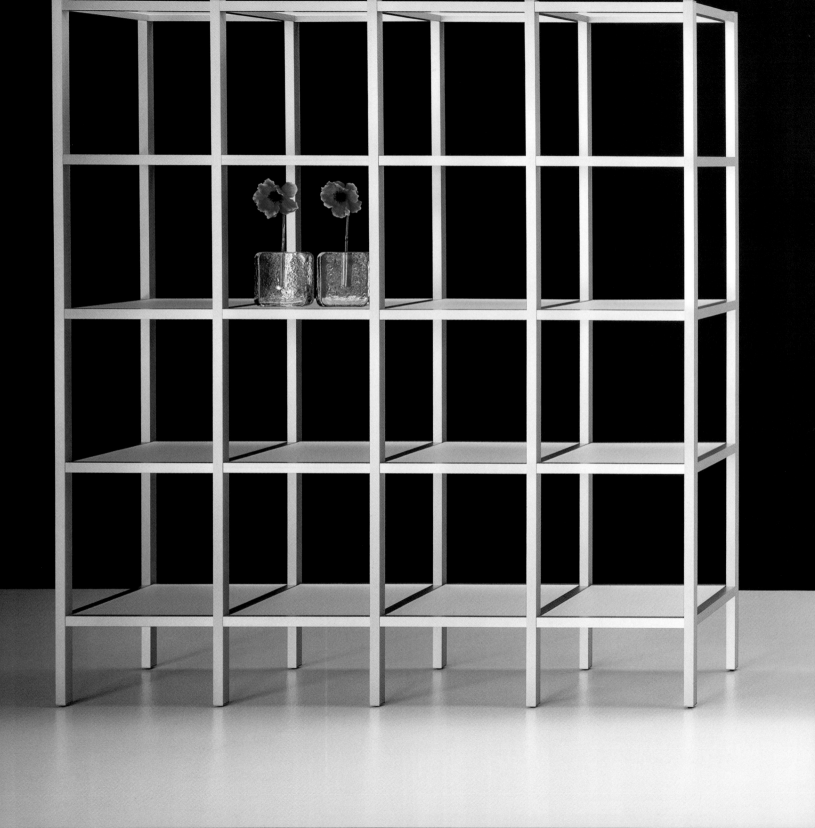

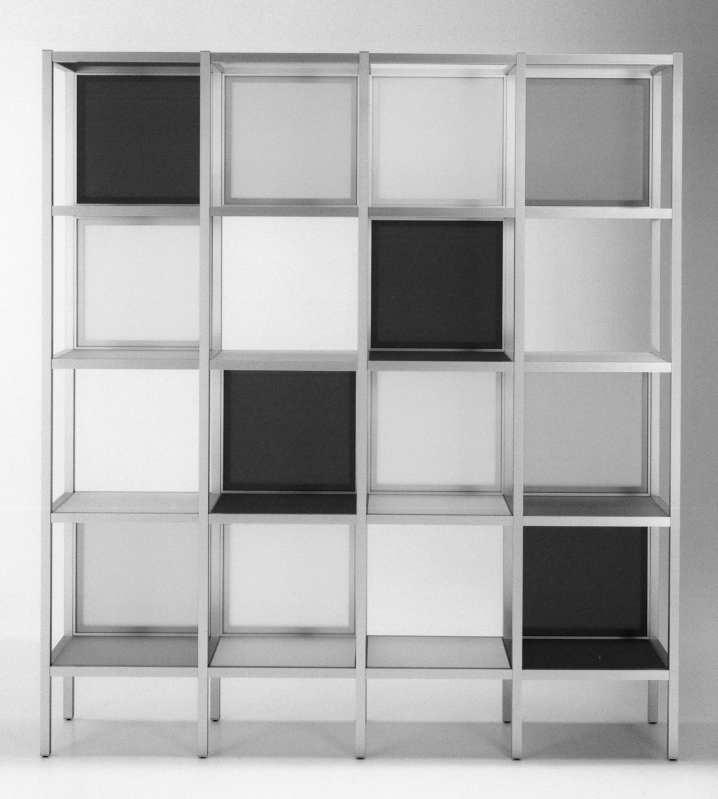

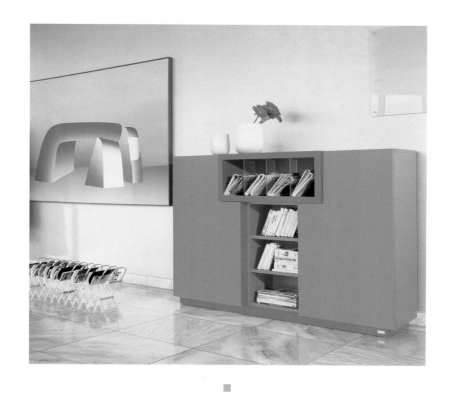

"At the beginning of the last century,
decoration was applied to everything,
from a beer stein to a door handle. In
this, Adolf Loos perceived a mixture of
reality and fantasy, which was highly
damaging to both of them. The principles
of design of objects for use should be
solely objective and determined by the
functions the object must fulfill."

A. Janik and S. Toulmin

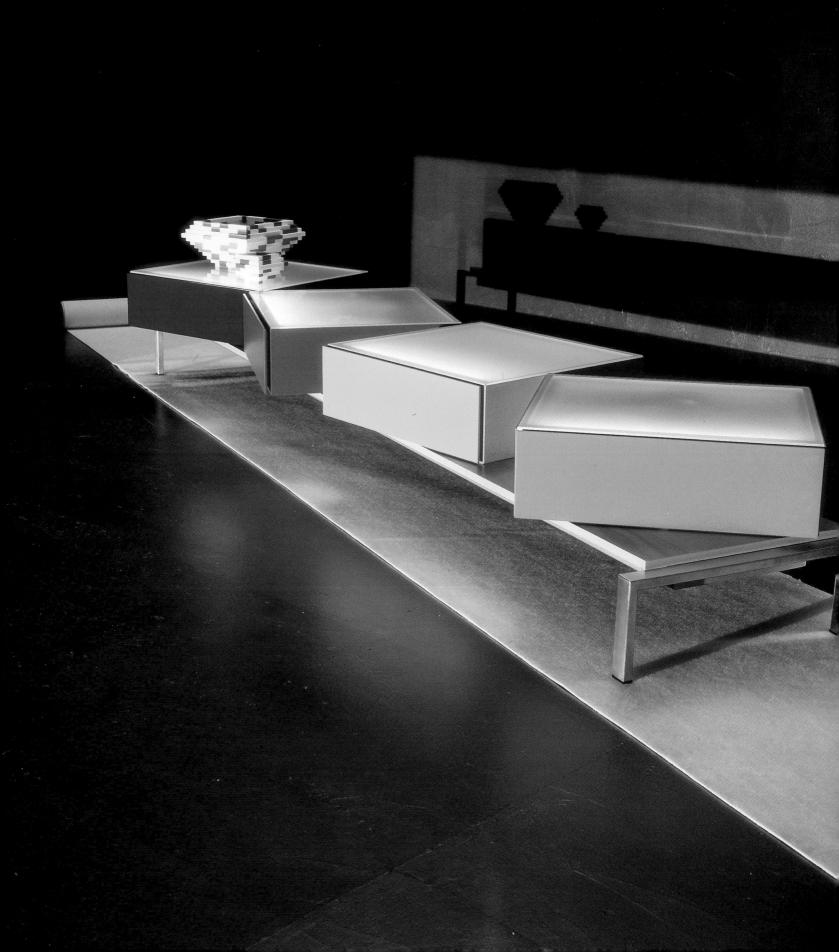

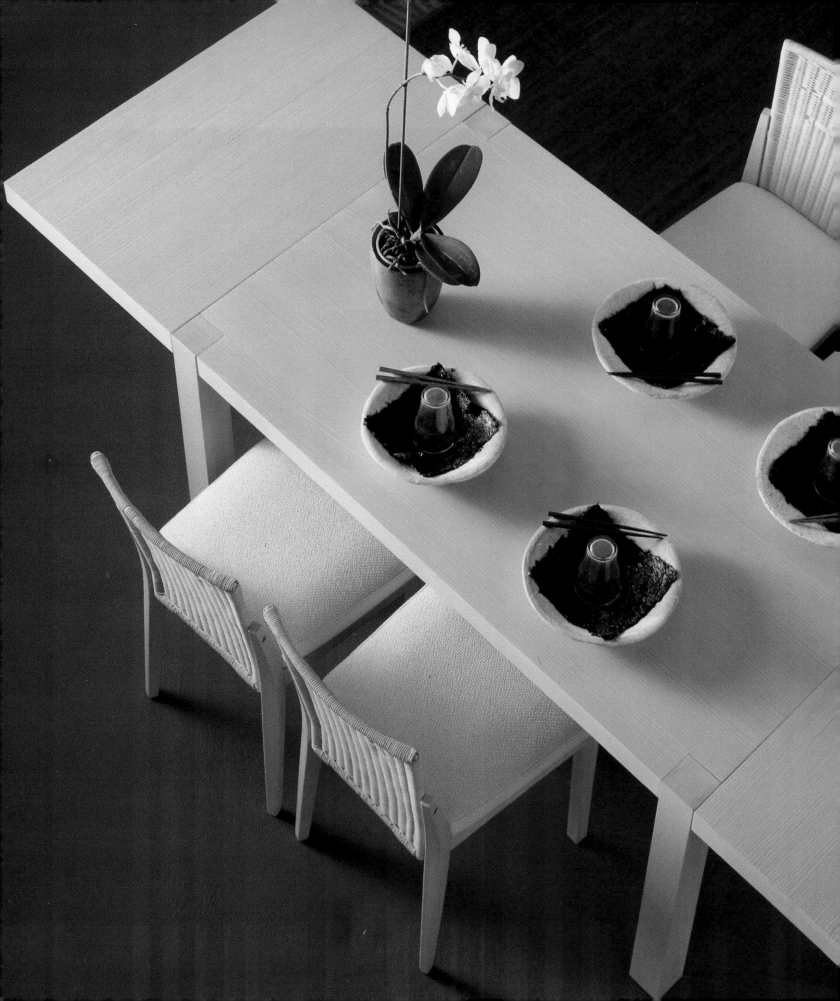

Minimalist art seeks to reference art itself, presenting, rather that representing. Through its defense of geometry, clarity, precision, and non-relational organization of the parts, minimalist art places the emphasis on the real, the material, the here and now. Frank Stella, one of its advocates, offers an easy summary of the movement's ideology referring to one of his paintings: "What you see is what you see".

The extension of the minimalist label to other forms of expression, such as music, cinema, dance, literature and architecture, makes it difficult to precisely define the movement. In general terms that might allow us to cover all the arts, the minimalist style is characterized by severity of means, clarity of form and simplicity of structure and texture.

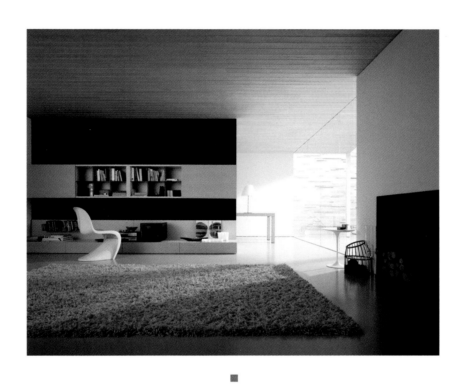

Color plays a vital role in the world
in which we live. When used correctly,
it can save on energy consumption.
When used erroneously, it can contribute
to global pollution.

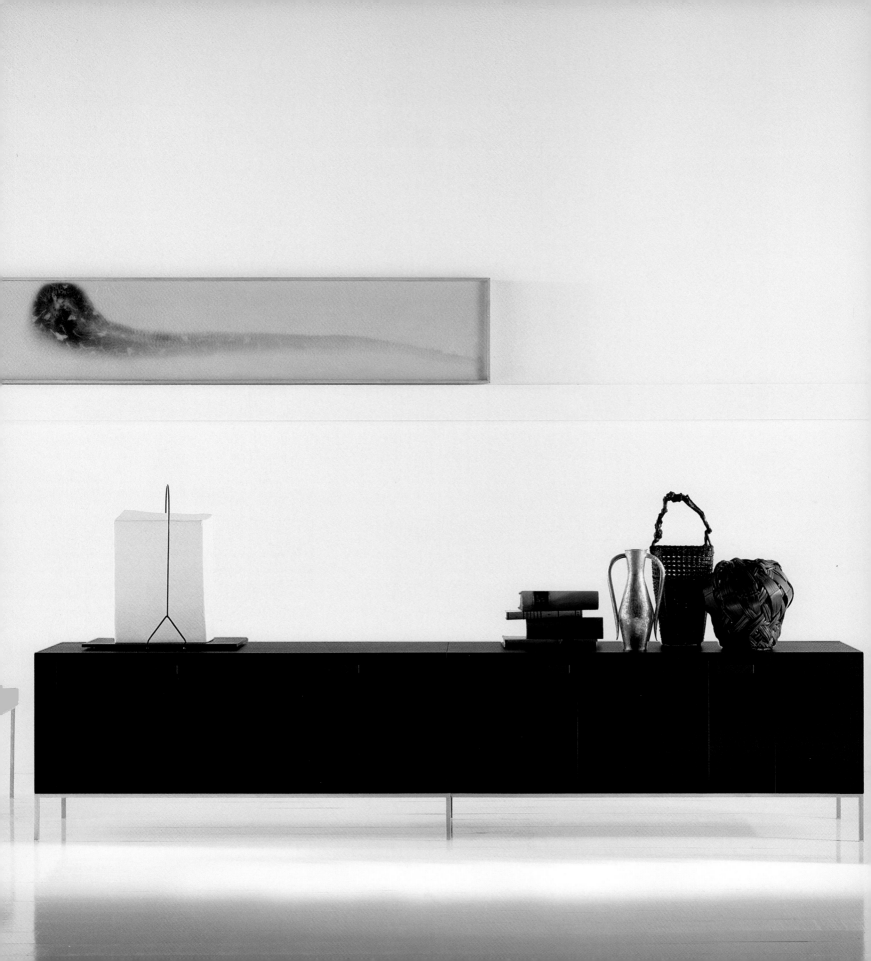

Minimalist artists use silence, repetition and the exposure of the medium to induce a kind of meditational receptivity in the spectator. Silence can be understood as space: quietness, emptiness, essence and absence create a space that induces passive meditation. In the visual arts, space is frequently used, whether through the absence of definite images on a blank canvas or through the air surrounding a sculpture in a museum. In this way, musicians, such as John Cage or Karlheinz, or plastic artists, such as Frank Stella, Dan Flavin or Donald Judd, manage to introduce into the audience's mind something that is almost impossible to achieve in an urban environment: silence, space and absence. As far as the method of repetition is concerned, it consists of the recurrence of similar patterns, as in the repetition of lines, with the same objective as the use of silence: to create a meditative space that does not fall into the trap of provoking boredom. Finally, the exposure of the medium supposes minimal technical complexity, in such a way that the artist simplifies the artistic method to such an extent that he reveals to the audience what is hidden behind "art." This method was applied to sculpture; works of art were taken down from their pedestals and placed directly on the floor of the exhibition hall in a way that spectators could walk around the piece with complete freedom. In this way, a new relationship between the artist and the audience was forged, in which the space that the sculpture occupied also became very important, changing the way in which art is contemplated. As a result of this change, sculpture acquired a new state of independence.

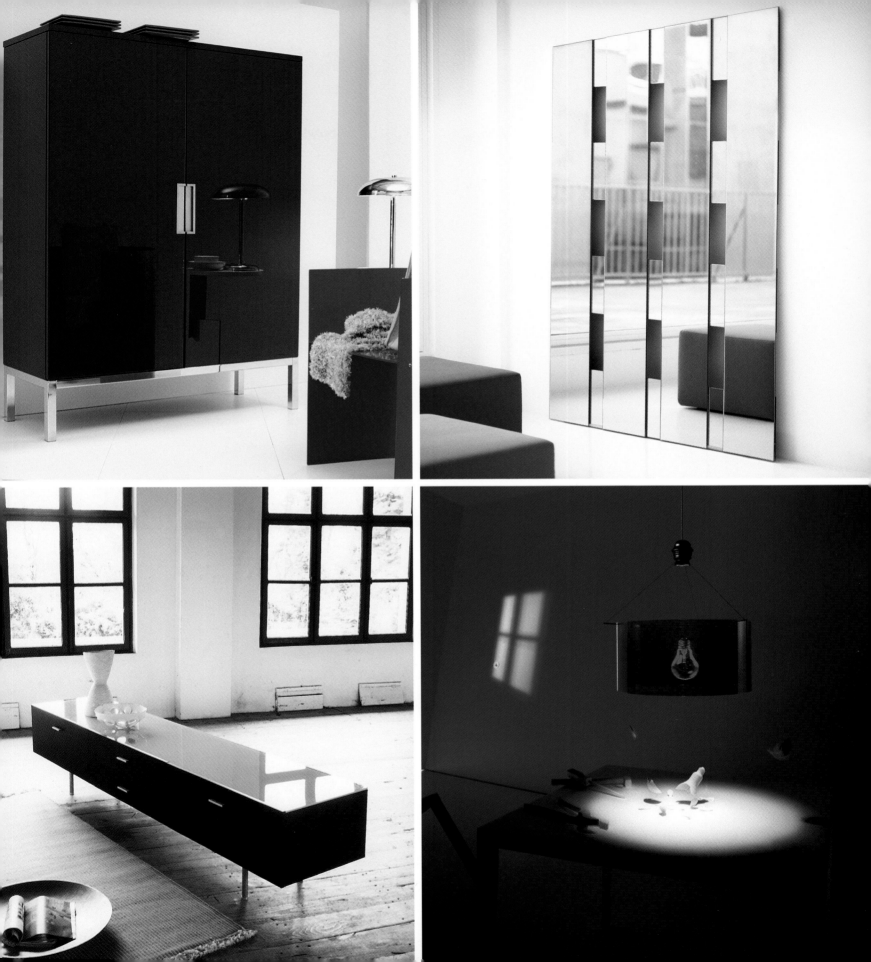

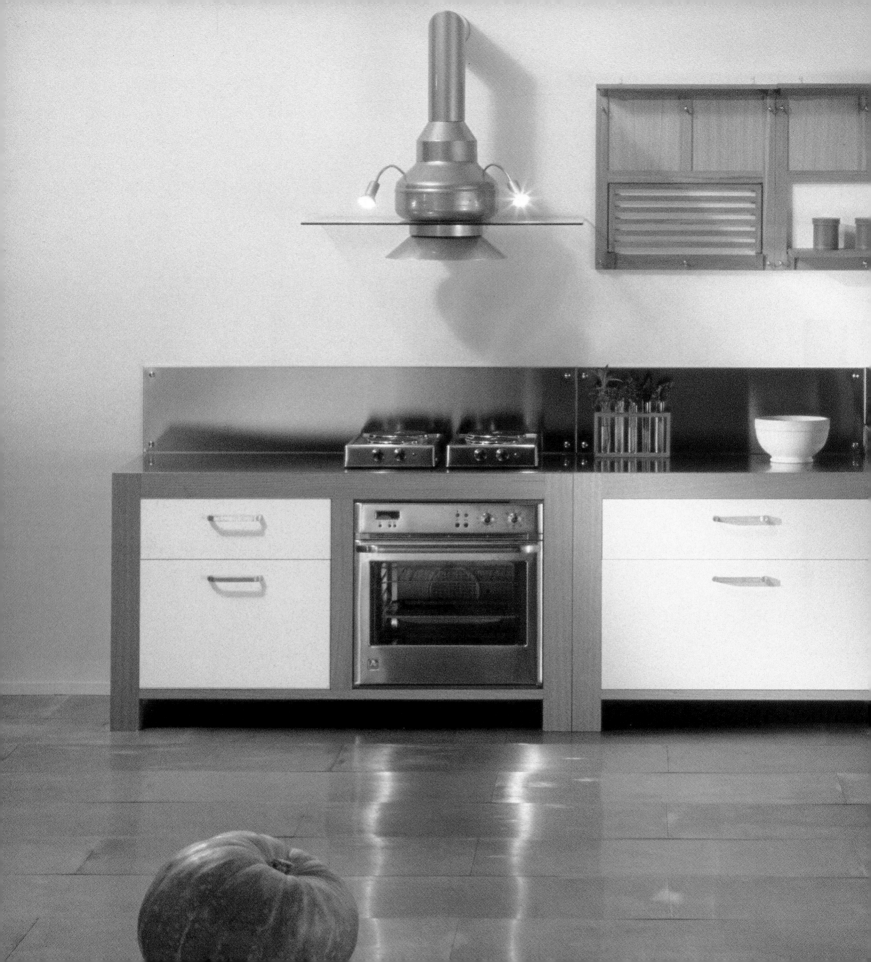

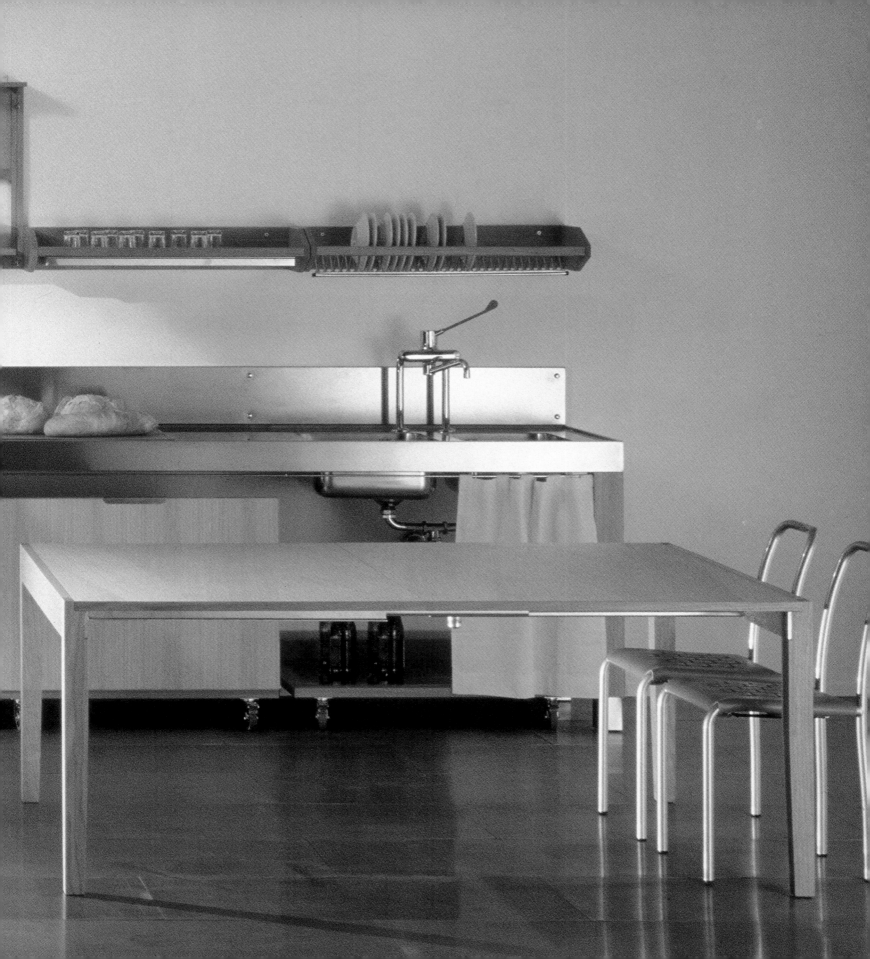

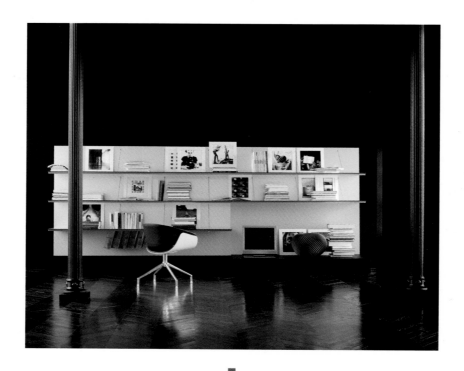

" A project for a piece of furniture
implies the design of an environment,
where the use of this piece, its position
and its relationship with the other pieces
of furniture are the means used to
participate in the daily rituals of
domestic behavior."

Antonio Citterio

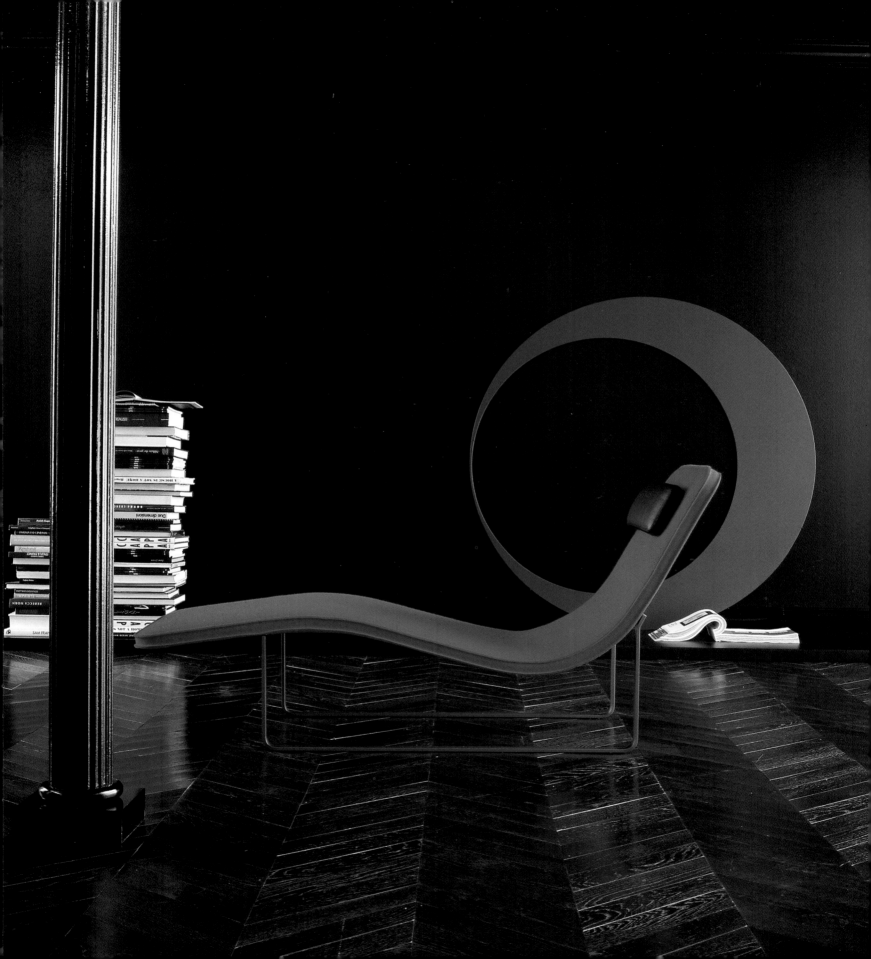

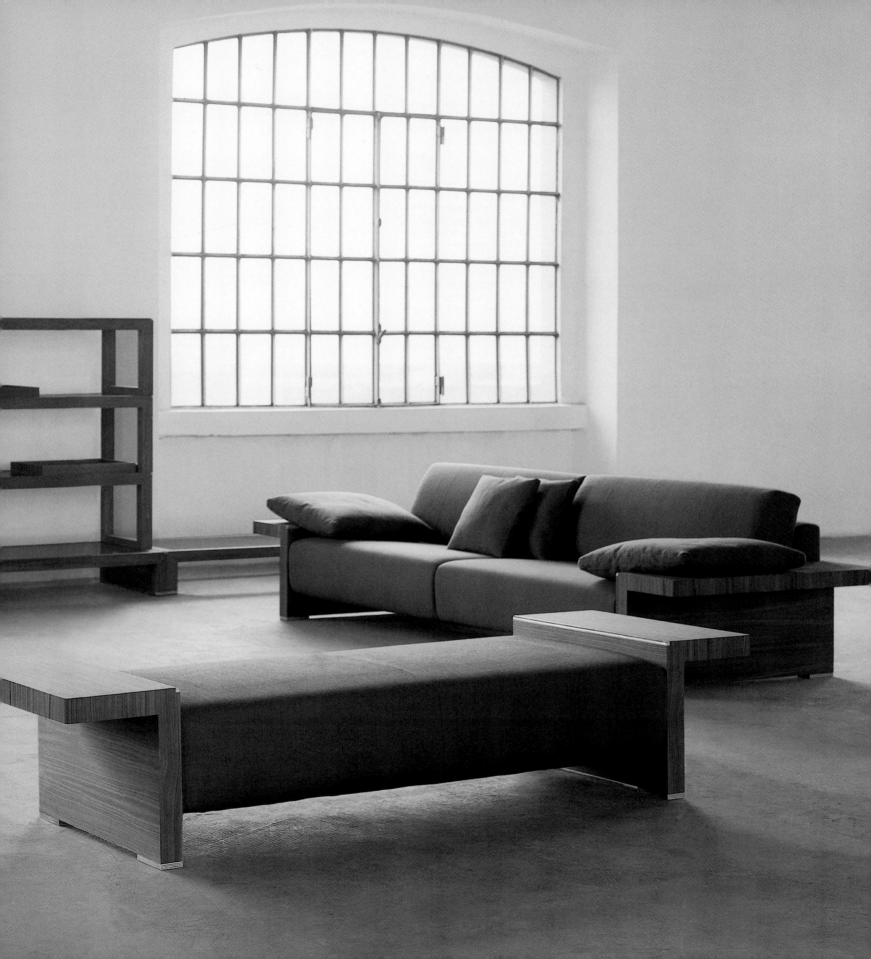

The minimalist movement broke other artistic conventions that were present at that moment. For example, the sculptor Donald Judd deliberately challenged the traditional artistic convention of originality by using industrial processes and materials, such as steel, concrete and plywood, in order to create large and hollow minimalist sculptures, mostly in the form of boxes, which he arranged in repeated simple geometric forms.

When one observes a relatively purist minimalist interior, the parallels between the interior and the artistic movement become obvious. One might even claim, that what began in the United States in the 60's as an artistic movement has been transformed into a way of life that has possibly become the best example of life imitating art.

Consequently, we can conclude that some proposals put forward by minimalist artists lie at the root of the conception of minimalist interiors. On one hand, in its idealistic aspect, the objective of neutralizing the values of a highly industrialized society remains. On the other hand, this objective is related to its practical application: the rejection of all that which is narrative, symbolic, mimetic, or fetishistic, so that significance is constructed by the spectator own perception. Silence, emptiness, quietness, space, absence, methodological simplification, independence with respect to tradition, geometry, and the importance of texture, qualities inherent in minimalist works of art, all find continuity in this new style of living.

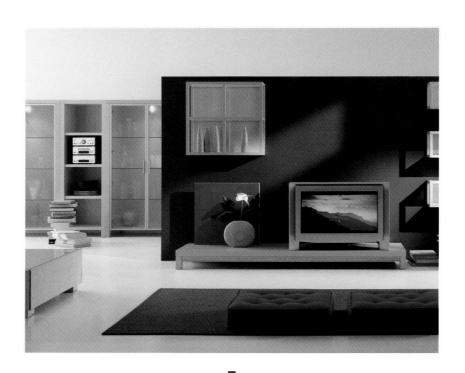

■

The concept "the form follows
the function" represents the desire
of the Modern Movement to replace
unnecessary objects with
indispensable forms.

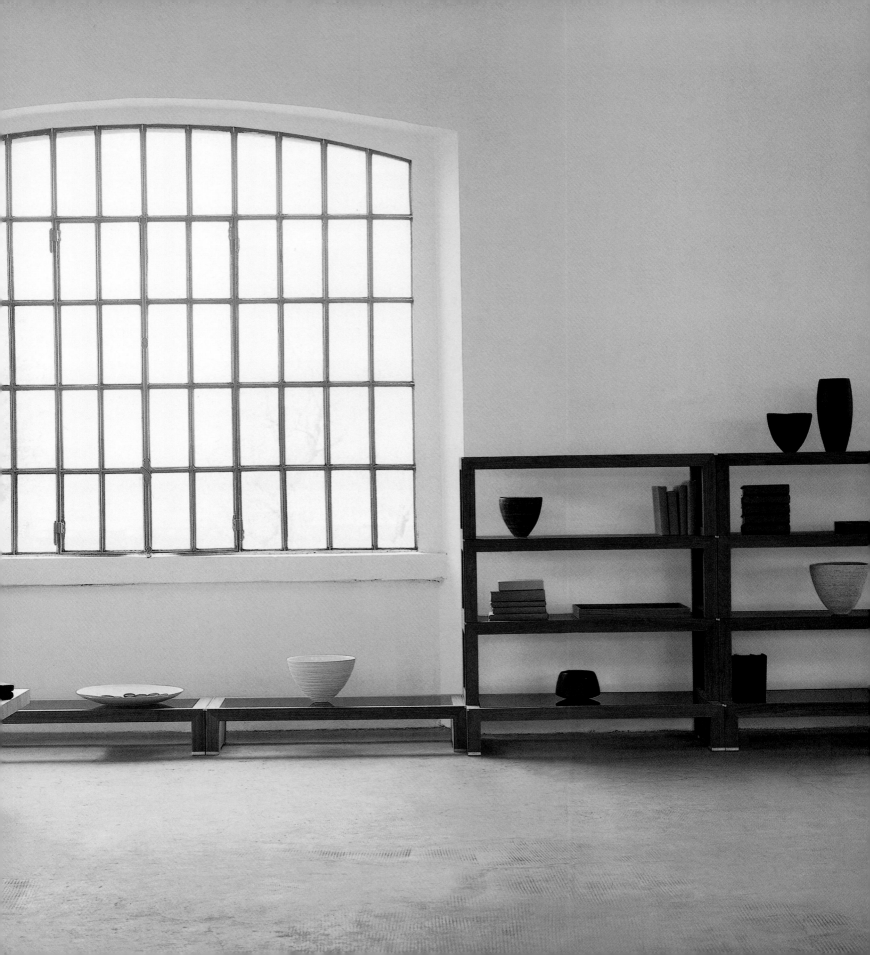

Within the final result of a work of art or a minimalist interior, an analogy can be seen: the essentiality of minimalism forces us to look into ourselves in order to try to discover why a particular shape or color is capable of transmitting such powerful emotion, independently of any rational context or secondary associations. In other words, both minimalist art and interiors are able to transmit emotion and aesthetic pleasure, derived from their manifesto of clarity and perfect order. Perhaps the success of minimalism, in both art and decoration, results from its skill at invoking the most universal passions through the austerity of the media used, challenging the march of time.

Minimalism & Zen

Clear precedents for Western minimalist interiors can be observed in certain concepts of some oriental philosophies, especially Zen Buddhism. In its quest for the essence of things, and its fleeing from disorder, the Zen philosophy is firmly rooted in the concept of minimalism. The Zen effort to eliminate everything superfluous, reaching a simplicity which allows greater concentration and deeper appreciation of everything that surrounds us, has turned into the minimalist dream of the 21st century.

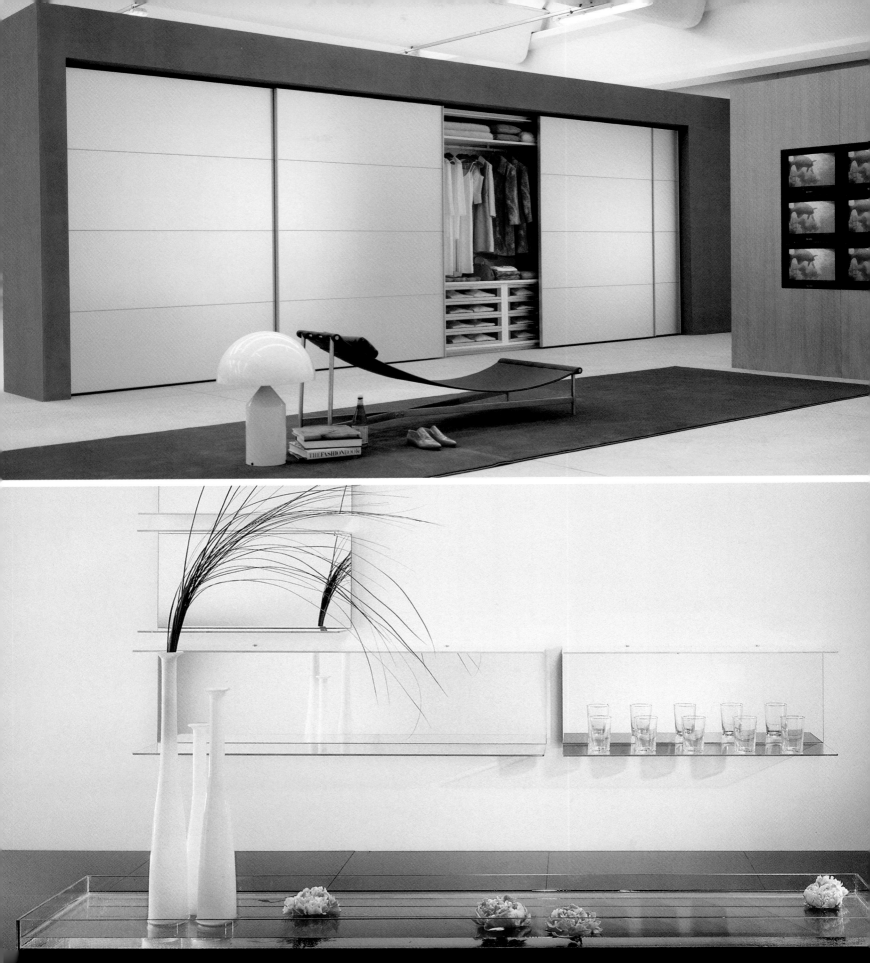

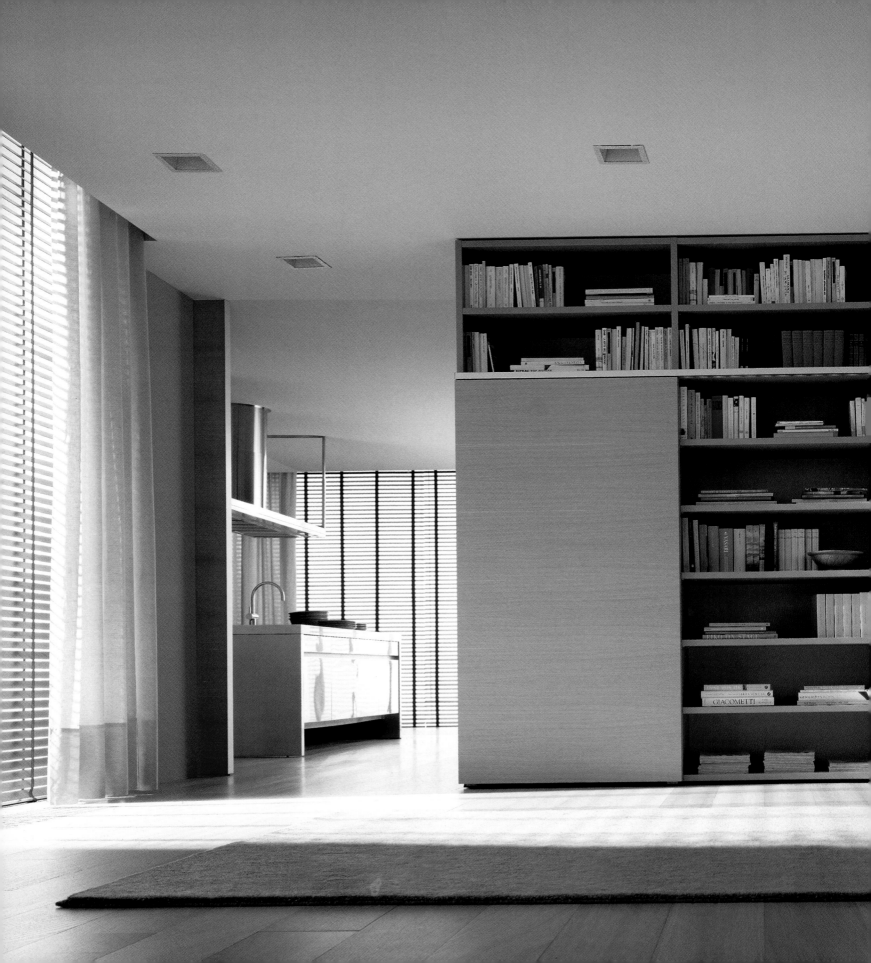

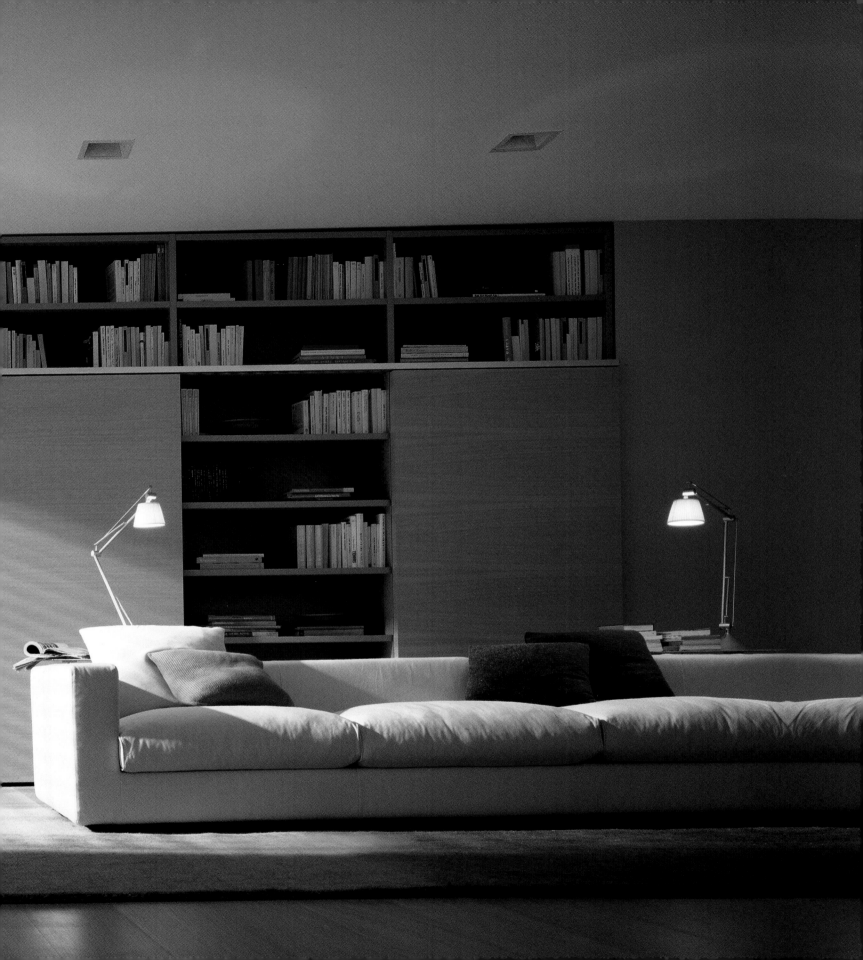

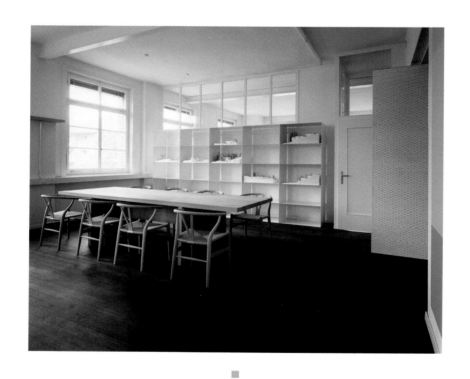

The geometric style of Bauhaus inspired
Minimalism during the sixties and
seventies, abandoning the aerodynamic
forms of the fifties.

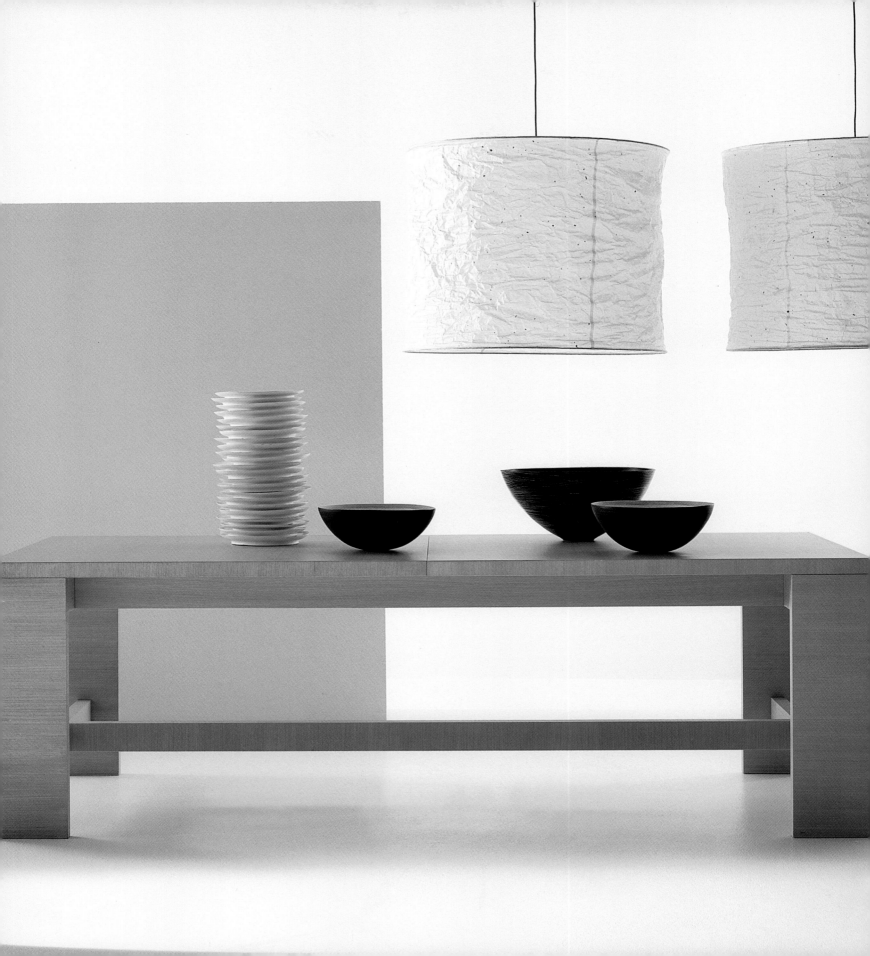

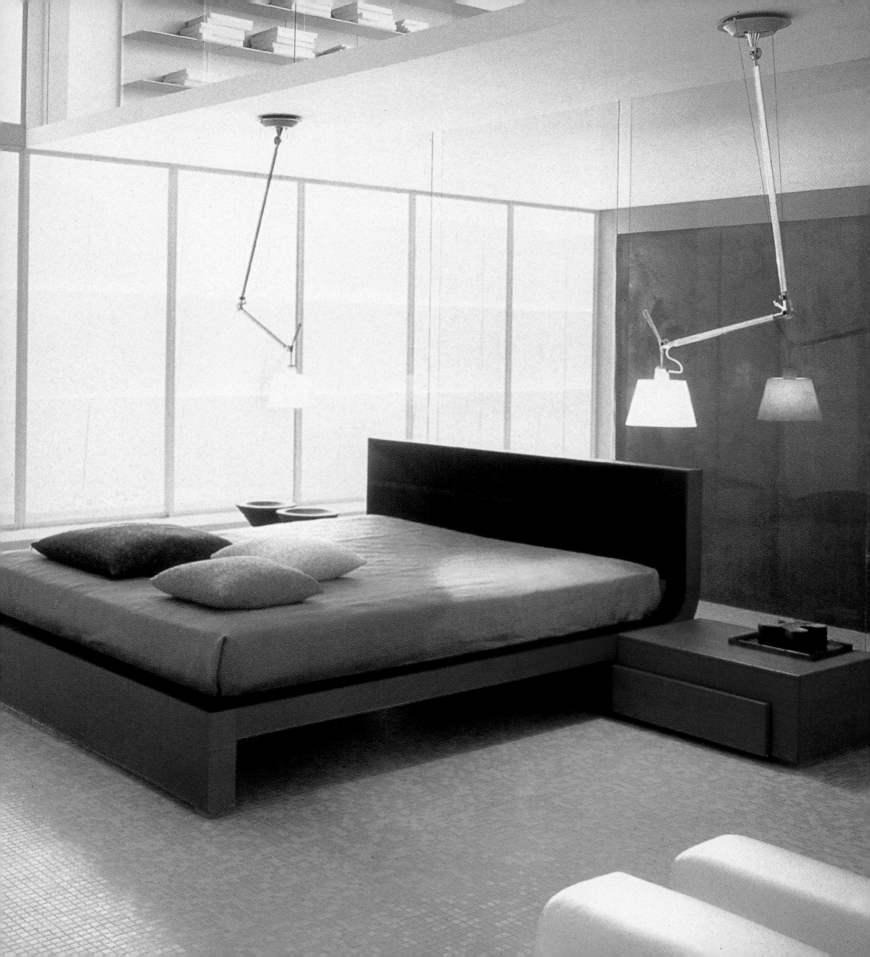

The Zen life style, of the essence reached when the unnecessary is eliminated, corresponds to the philosophy that permeates traditional Japanese houses. The austerity of these houses is not seen as deprivation, but rather a rescue of the inner being by banishing disorder, ostentation, and vanity from our environment.

This austerity is perhaps best expressed in the purest style of tea house architecture, whose construction methods, later extended to other types of buildings, gave rise to the important style known as *"Sukiya-zukuri."* However, the original approach claimed not to focus on the building materials but on the emptiness that they contained, resulting in the definition of tea houses as "houses of the soul" or "houses of emptiness". In fact, one can state that this kind of architectural style, principally developed by Zen monks at the end of the 16th century, is the only one that we can find before the arrival of the Modern Movement, that rejects the incorporation of decorative elements, ostentation and complexity infavor of simplicity and restraint.

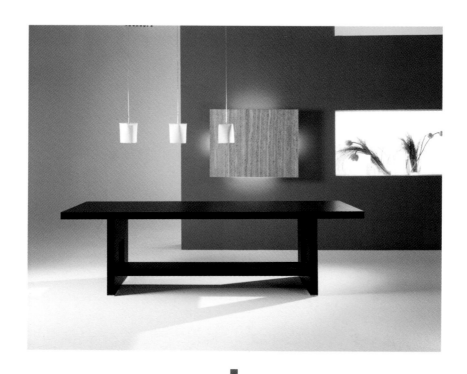

The reason why one empty space works
and another does not could be a question
of a few millimeters in one direction or
another.

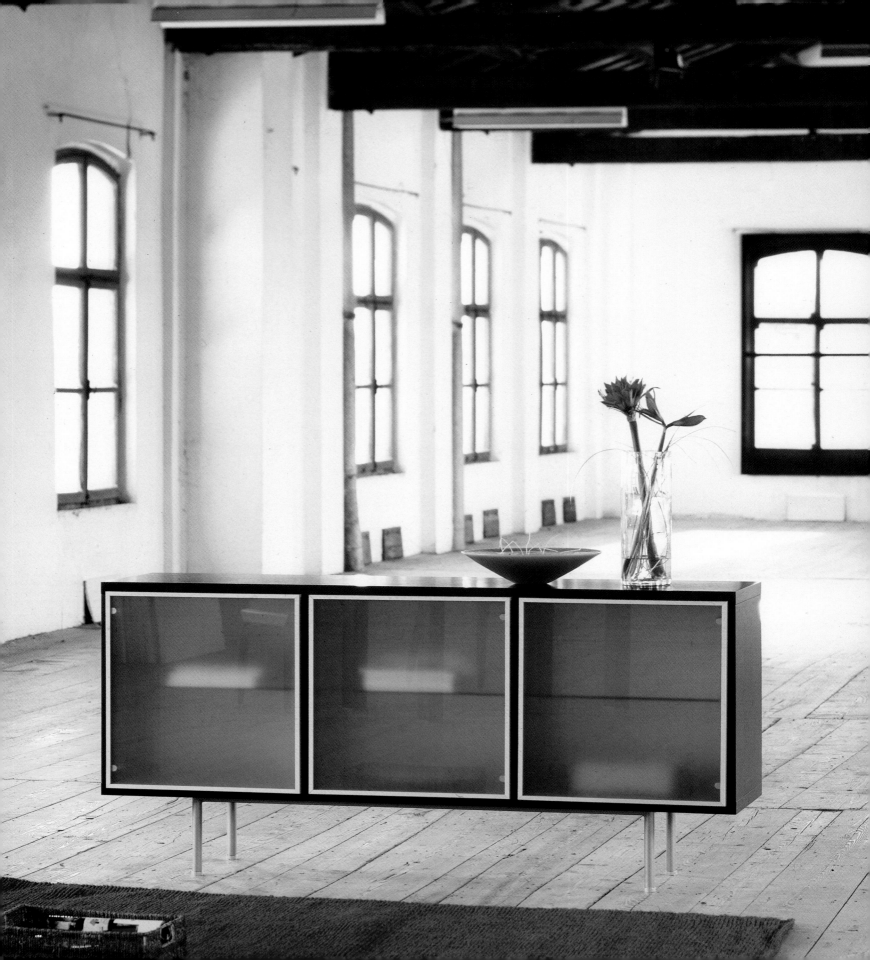

In the construction of tea houses, known as *chashitsu*, the form derived directly from the function (something that reminds us of one of the main postulates of functionalism). On the one hand, they were designed to unite a small group of people (maximum six) in a relaxed environment around a cup of tea. On the other, their purpose was to aid in the achievement of a profound spiritual satisfaction through the act of drinking tea and silent contemplation. Some Zen monks brought specific innovations to the tea ceremony. Amongst them, we find Rikyu (1522-91), considered to be the founder of the ceremony as it is practiced in Japan today. Rikyu thought that the proper spirit for the ceremony consisted of four elements: harmony, reverence, purity and tranquility. He believed that, in general, man was too egotistical and worried about protecting himself from others and the world at large. For this reason, Rikyu wanted to create, through the art of tea, an atmosphere of such tranquility that men would feel no threat. Based on this tranquility, each person would obtain an intuitive sense of the harmony that can be found in nature and the purity of the heart provided by the understanding of this harmony. This purity would bestow on the individual such a state of well-being that it would result in respect for all of nature's creations. Consequently, the tea ceremony is a good way of escaping from the wrath and jealousy of everyday life, from the need for self-defense, finally reaching the spirit that transcends the form. What is created in the *chashitsu* is a poem of eternity in the shape of a building.

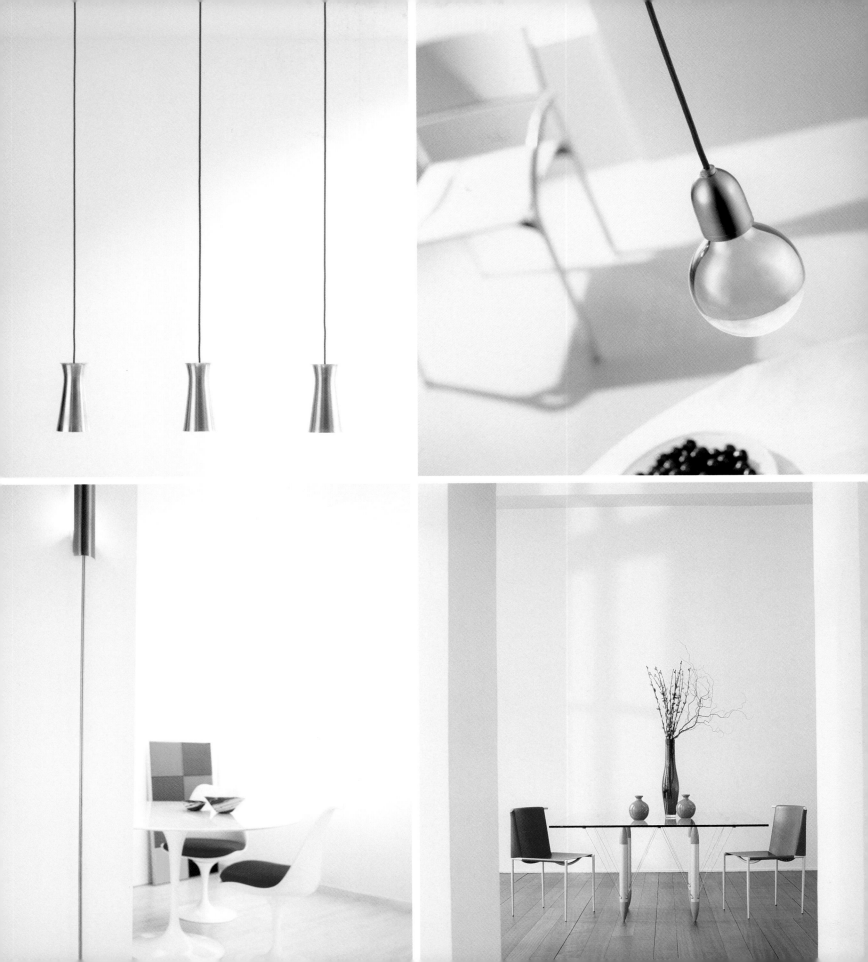

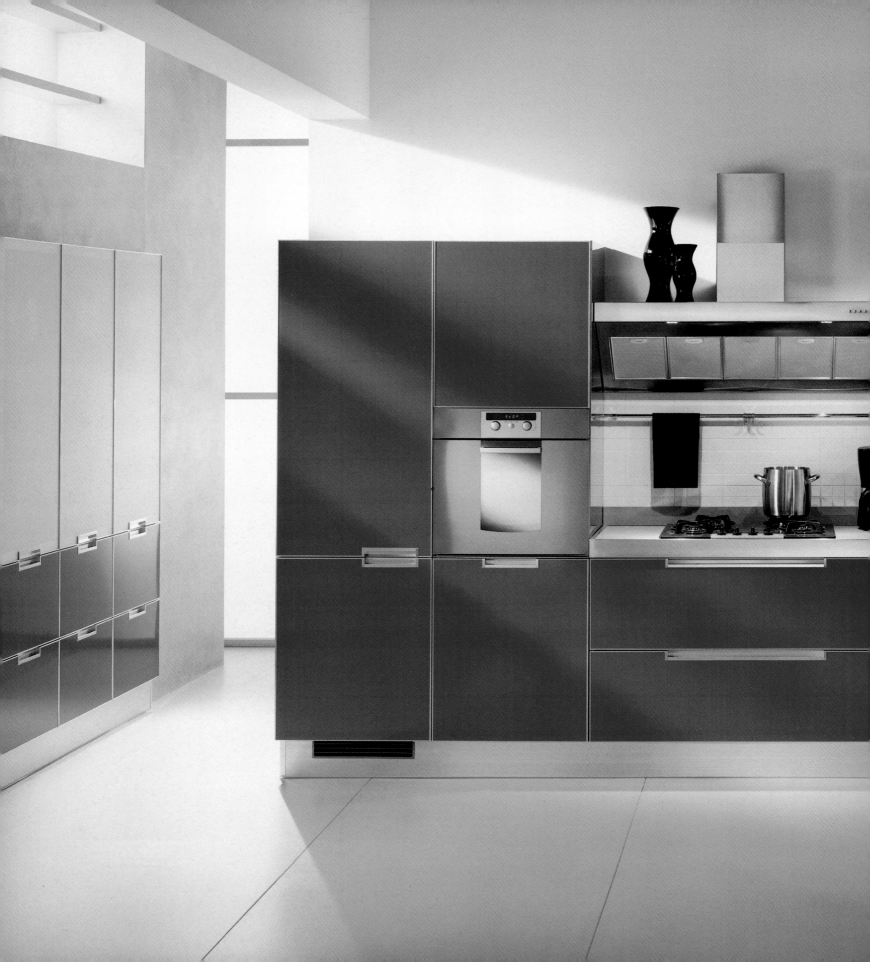

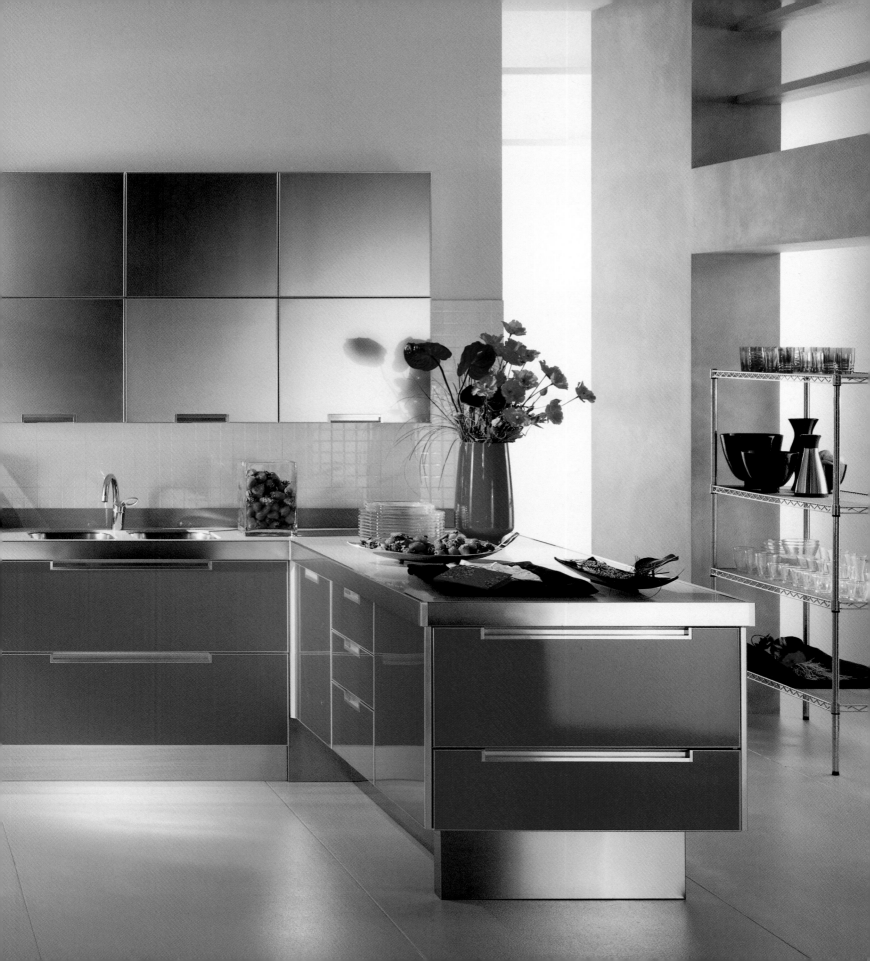

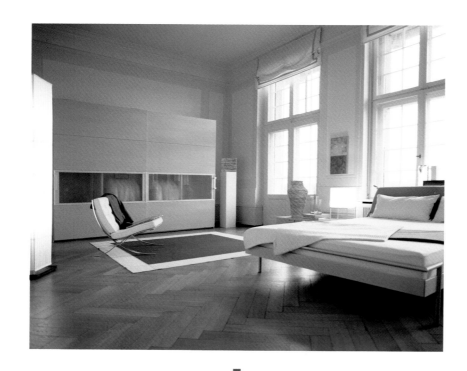

"...Furniture, including the walls which
separate rooms, are not compact,
monumental, apparently or really fixed;
but they are vaporous pieces which
appear to have sprouted in the room,
as if someone had drawn them."

Marcel Breuer, 1928

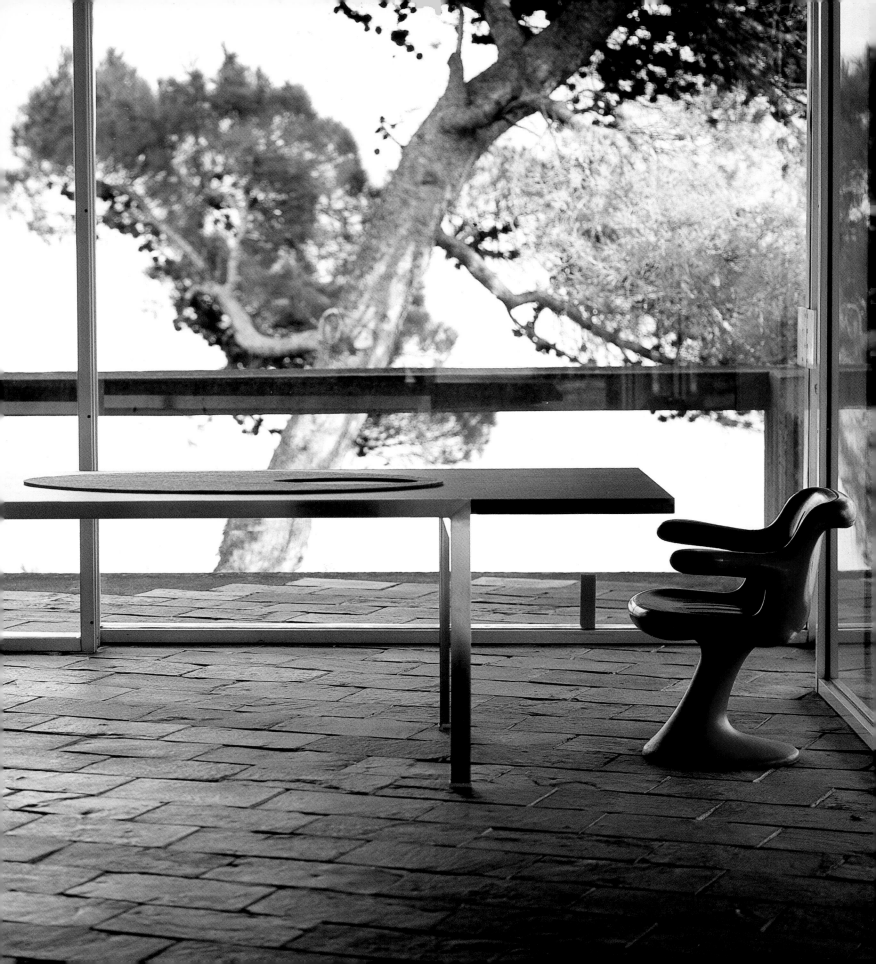

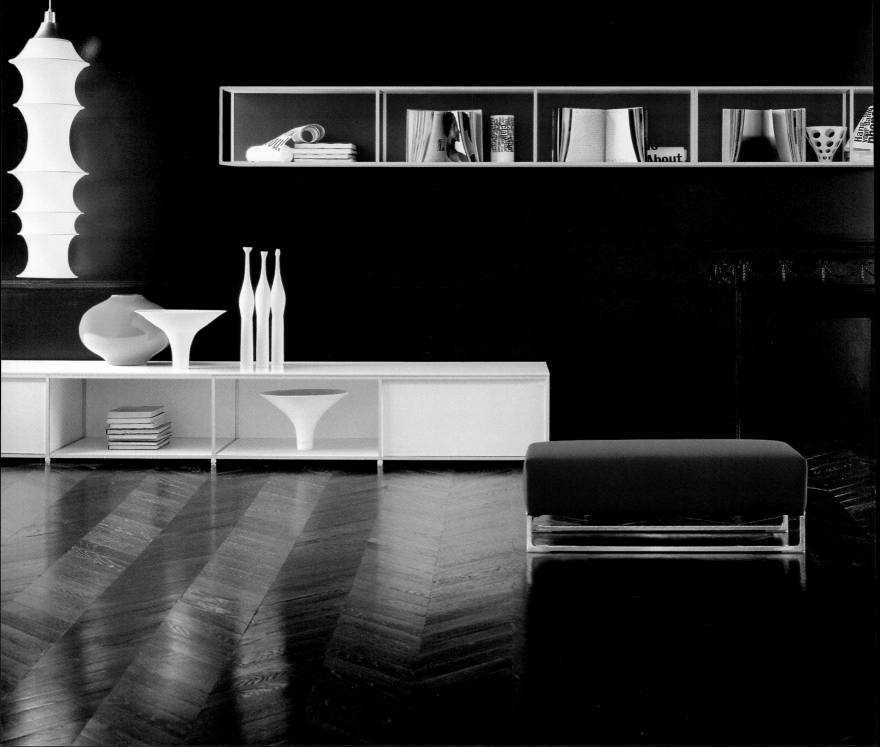

Another surprising example of the effect of the empty spaciousness that impregnates the tea houses can be found in the classic rock gardens, where the spaced stones underline absence. In both cases, the richness of the simplicity, the fascination for absence, and the respect for detail are evident. Minimalism is a resource at the disposal of today's society and that allows us to get closer to this particular aesthetic, absorbing its capacity to find transcendence in simplicity.

To clarify this "transcendent simplicity", it is necessary to make clear another concept inherent in the Zen aesthetic: the words *sabi* and *wabi*. *Wabi and Sabi* refer not only to the quest for the strictest or most "puritanical" simplicity, but also signifies freedom from anger, from envy and from anxiety. *Wabi* can also be understood as an element of renouncement and absence, interpreted in a positive way. When an interior is created with *wabi* and *sabi*, the inhabitant relates intimately with his environment, filling the empty spaces and finishing the composition in his mind, so it becomes a part of him and he a part of it.

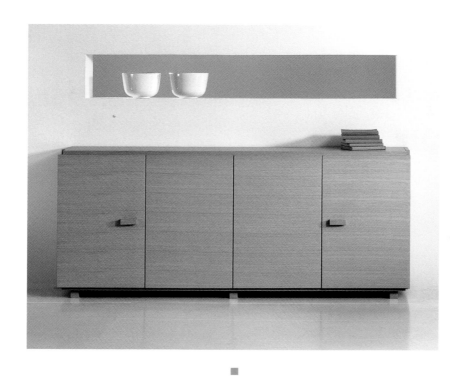

"One explanation for the richness of simplicity could be that architecture which does not refer to anything outside itself, which does not appeal to the intellect, automatically gives priority to direct experience, the sensory experience of space, material and light."

Hans Ibelings

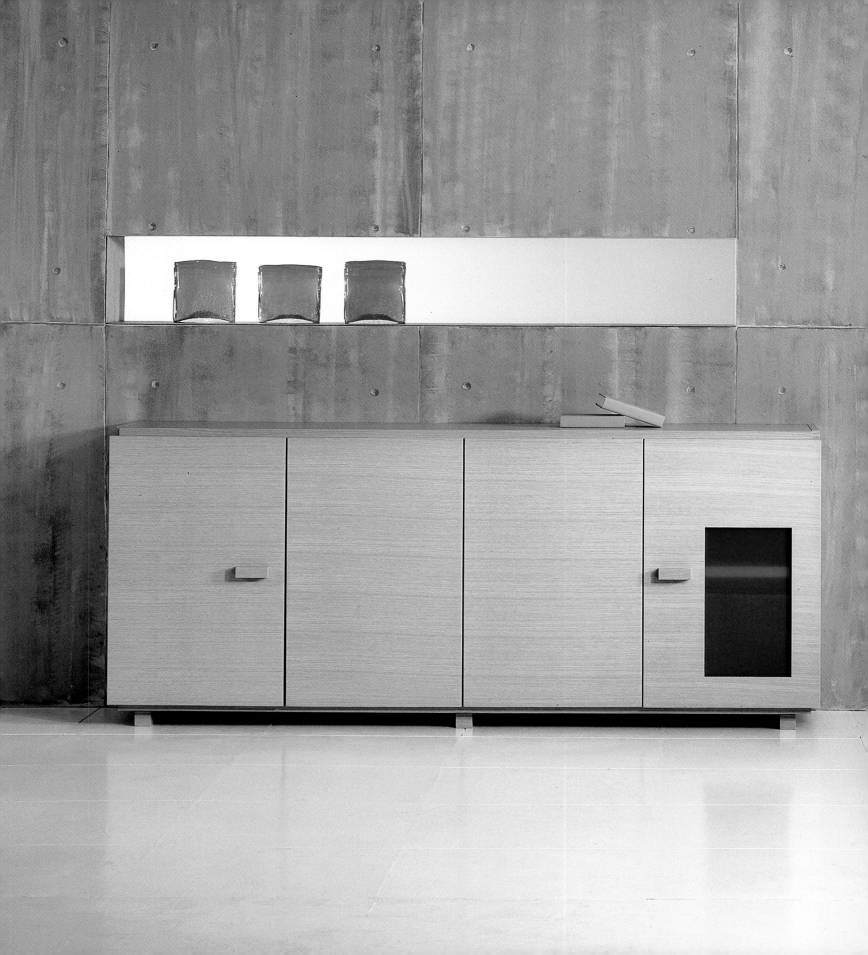

Some of the modern architects who have featured most prominently in history, such as Frank Lloyd Wright or Mies van der Rohe, found a clear source of inspiration in the concept of spaciousness developed by traditional Japanese architecture, or *Sukiya-zukuri*. This vision conceptualizes space not as defined by walls and ceilings, but as something independent that's value is its own emptiness. Moreover, within Zen Buddhism, it is often said that the nature of all things is empty (*shunya*), but this emptiness (*shunyata*) is not the same as nothingness, because it designates the identity of everything. In this way, this kind of architectural expression and other forms of visual arts, are not just a reflection of but the material incarnation of this spiritual emptiness that the Buddhists, and one might also dare to say the minimalists, want to reach.

Looking to this tendency of Buddhist thinking, which has dominated Japanese thought for almost a thousand years, speaks to the need to find new means of expression that would introduce spirituality and calm into the frenetic and saturated style of contemporary Western life. Without achieving the austerity and extreme emptiness of the traditional tea houses, we may try to remove all that is not necessary from our homes, and so attain the atmosphere of profound tranquility created by the master Rikyu in the tea ceremony; a state that can help us to learn more about ourselves and to feel in peace with the outside world. The results of this are interiors where we can enjoy the present, that transmit balance and order, that eliminate vanity through their simplicity and that are lasting and eternal, resistant to the passing of different fashions and times.

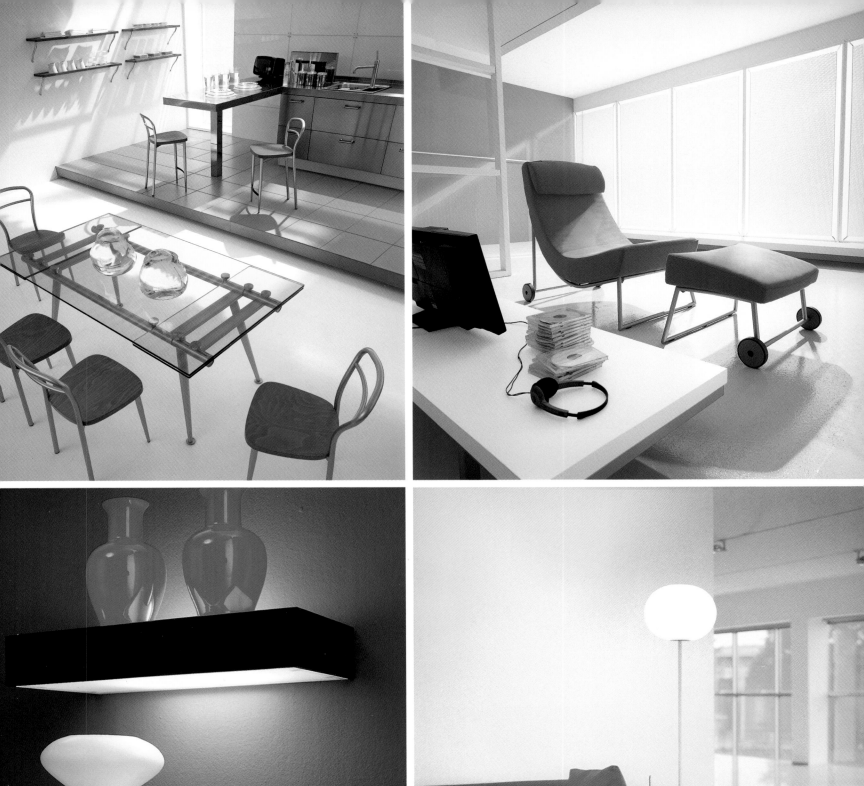
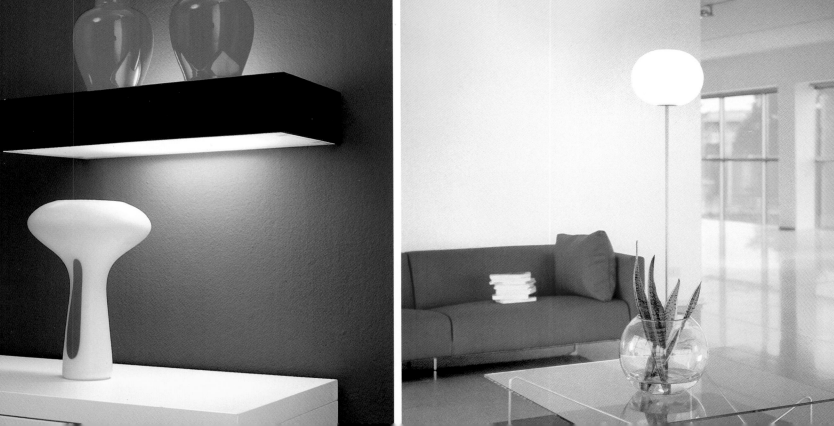

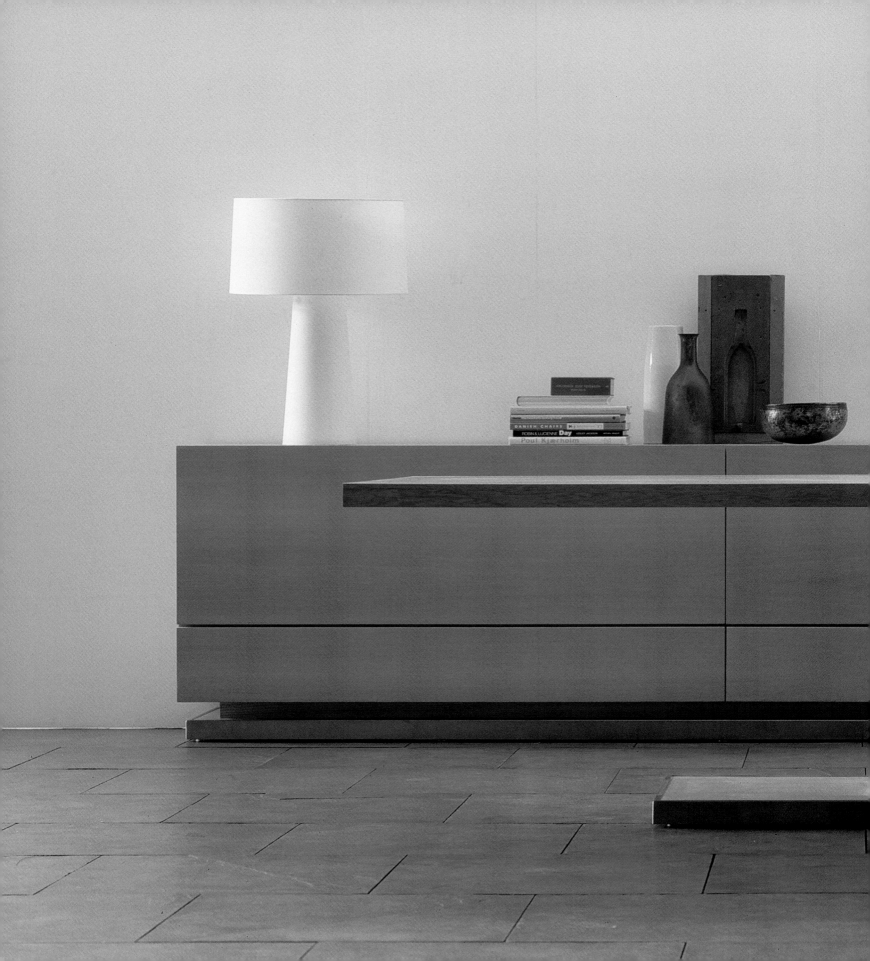

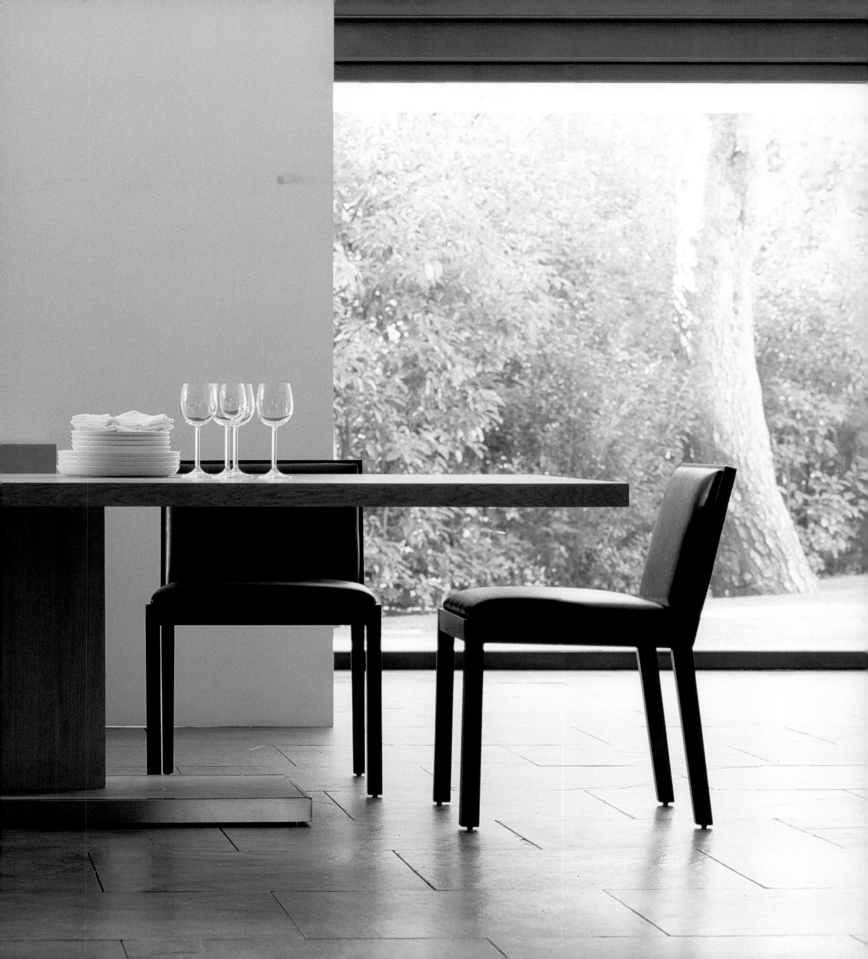

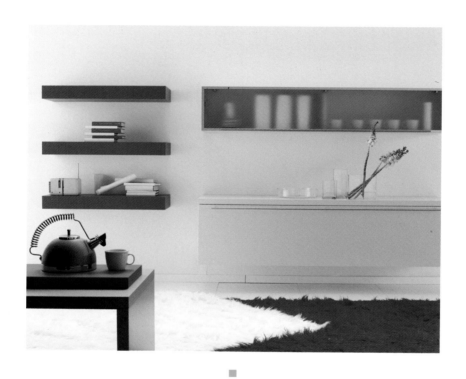

"Cultural evolution is equivalent to the
elimination of ornaments from all
articles used on a daily basis."

Adolf Loos

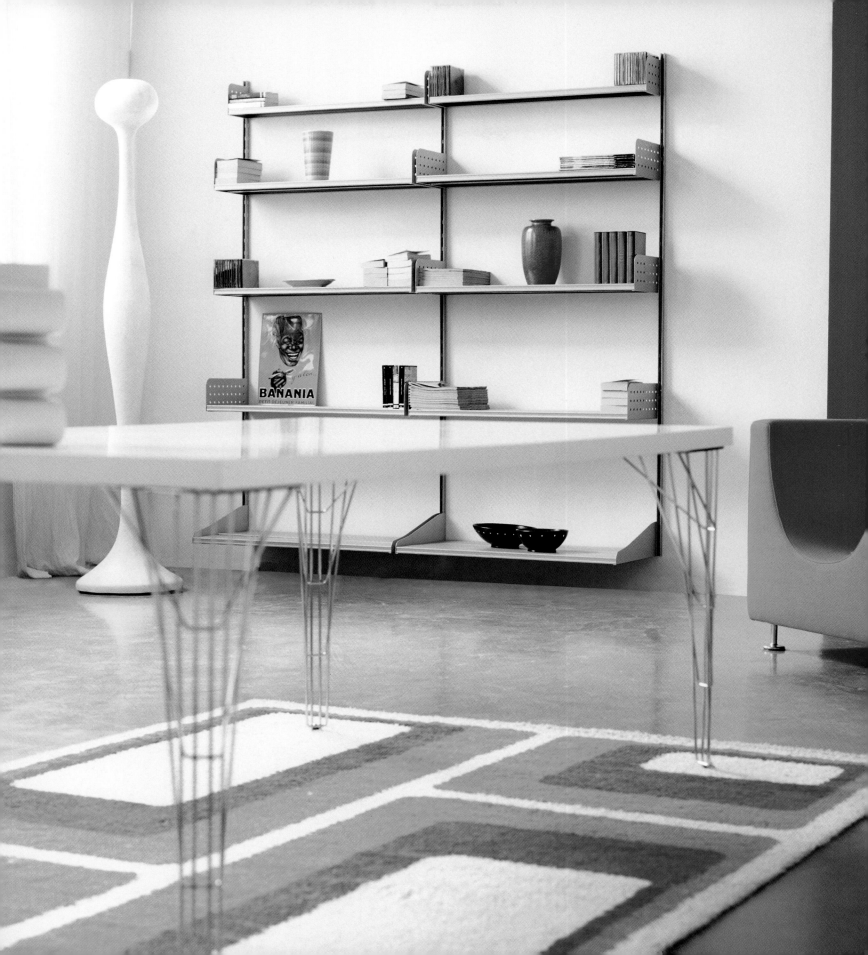

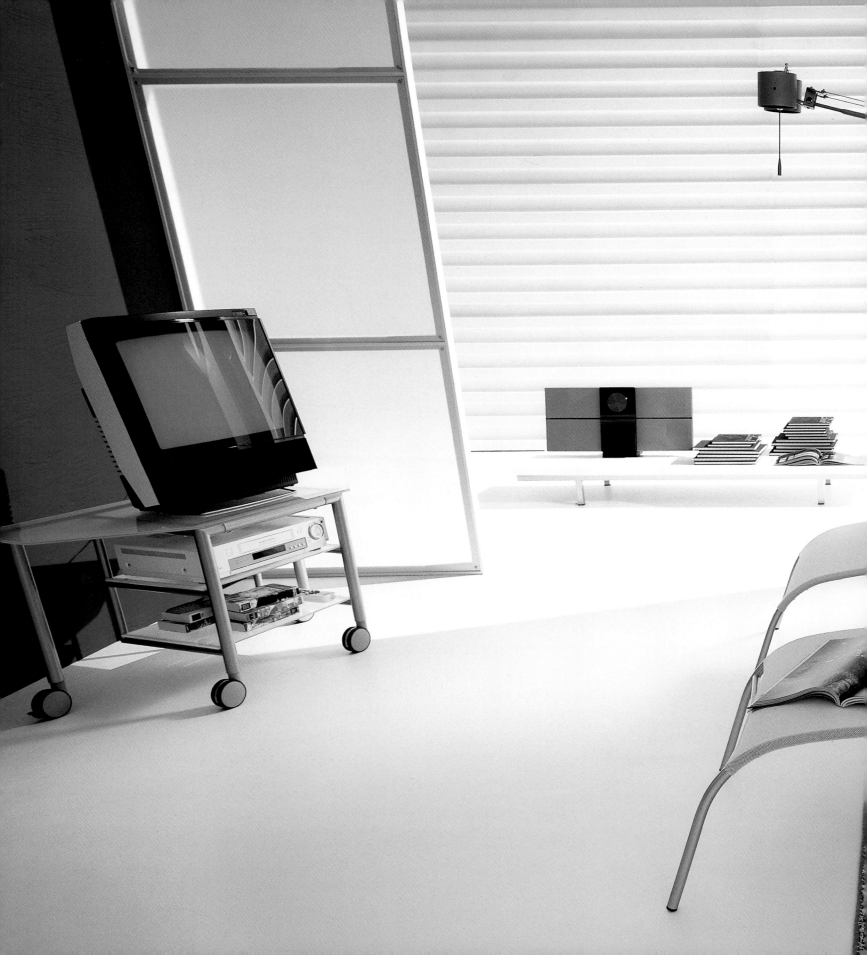

Interiors & Color: Concepts

Color & Perception

One could say that color is the essence of light and that light is the essence of life. Color perception is a subjective experience, due to the fact that it is not a material attribute, but a sensation produced by the reflection of light, which is then transmitted to the brain by the eye. Thus, the color of an object is the result of the change experienced by light when it is reflected, and white light, as we see it, is the integration of all the colors of the spectrum. If we see the material white, this means that the material reflects all light. If we see a color in particular, this means that its surface reflects the corresponding wavelengths for that color and that it absorbs the rest. If we see black, all the light is being absorbed.

The perception of color provokes different reactions in each person, depending on a number of interrelated factors that are generally associated with cultural inheritance and experience. Amongst these factors, certain ones stand out: chromatic relations (the perception of a tone depends on its relationship with the surrounding tones); surface relations (the influence of the size of a colored surface); texture; symbolic, cultural and emblematic values; and optical effects (or chromatic illusions).

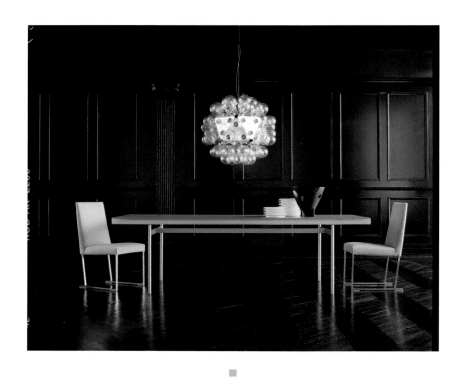

The relation of values, saturations and
the warmth or coldness of pure colors
can cause prominent differences in our
perception of color.

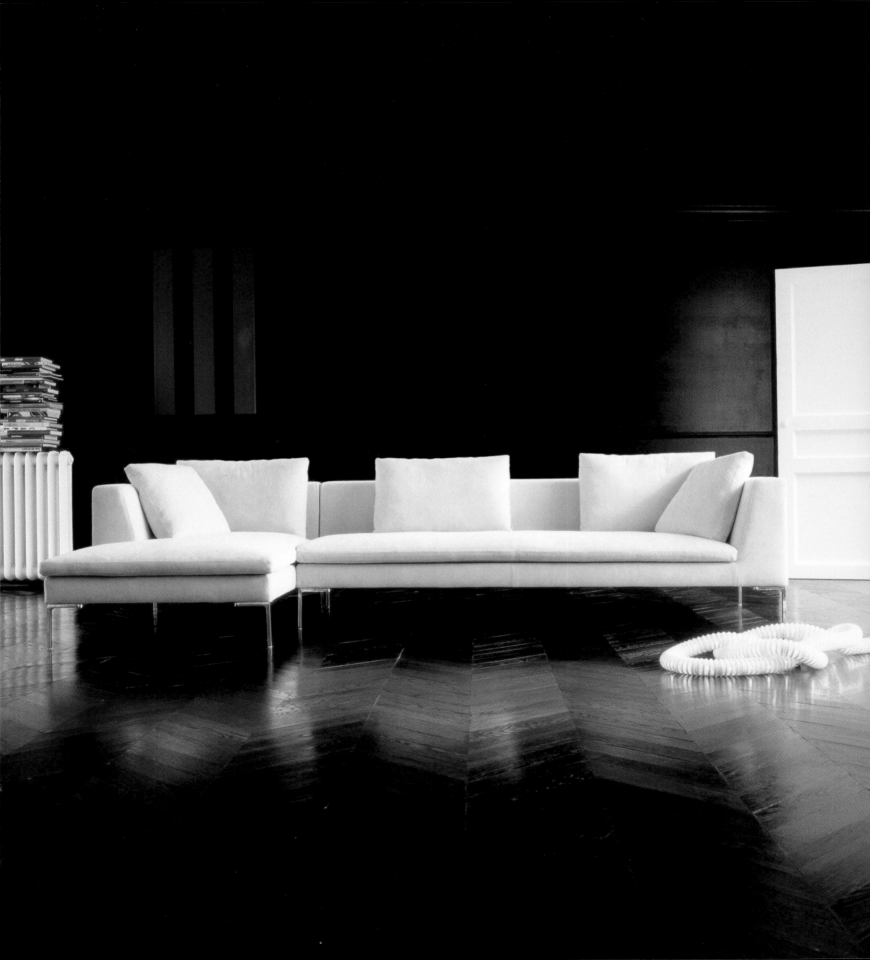

The way in which a surface reflects, absorbs or transmits light and the way in which the colors and textures surrounding it influence its color, helps us to determine an object's shape and position. The same tone combined with different surfaces or materials, such as metal, wood, cotton, velvet, linoleum, etc, can appear to be completely different. For example, a table lacquered in bright red will reflect light and its color will be intensified while the same red on plain cloth will be comparatively duller.

On the other hand, as far as the symbolic value of color is concerned, one of the most important attributes that affects the decoration of interiors is the color thermic sensation which is the fact that some tones are perceived as warm (yellows, reds and oranges) and others as cold (blues, greens and violets). The temperature of the color directly affects the perception of space of a room because it is thought that warm colors advance and move closer to the observer while cold colors recede and appear to move away.

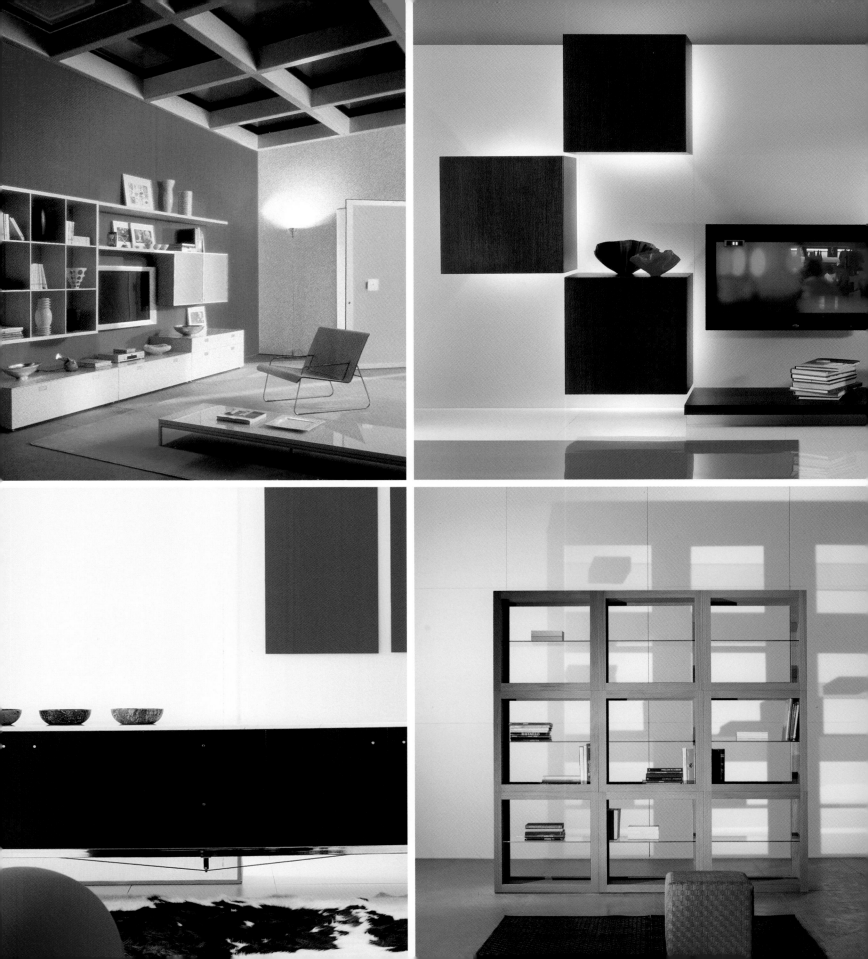

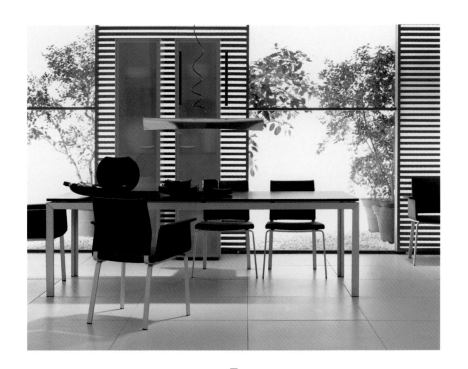

"Objects, after Postmodernism, will
never be as transparent as in the projects
of early industrial modernity, despite the
fact that they are as discreet as they
used to used to be. There must be
something in objects that invites us to
reflect ourselves in the sensory qualities
of that which we have before us."

Marcello Ziliani

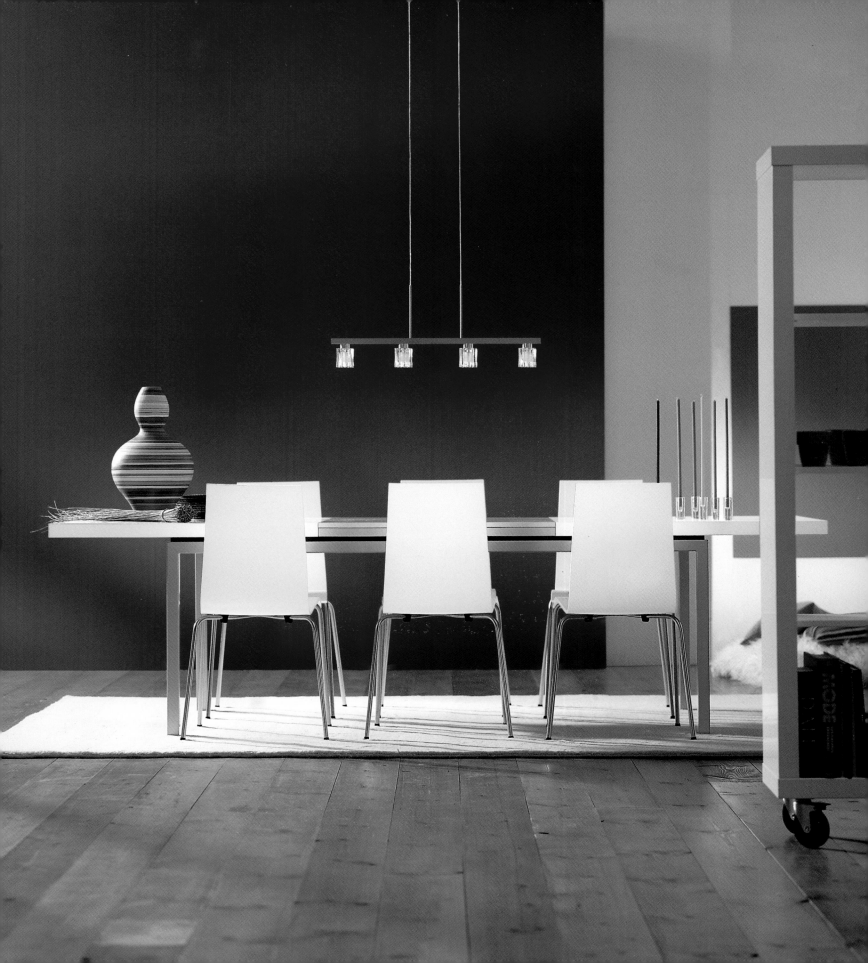

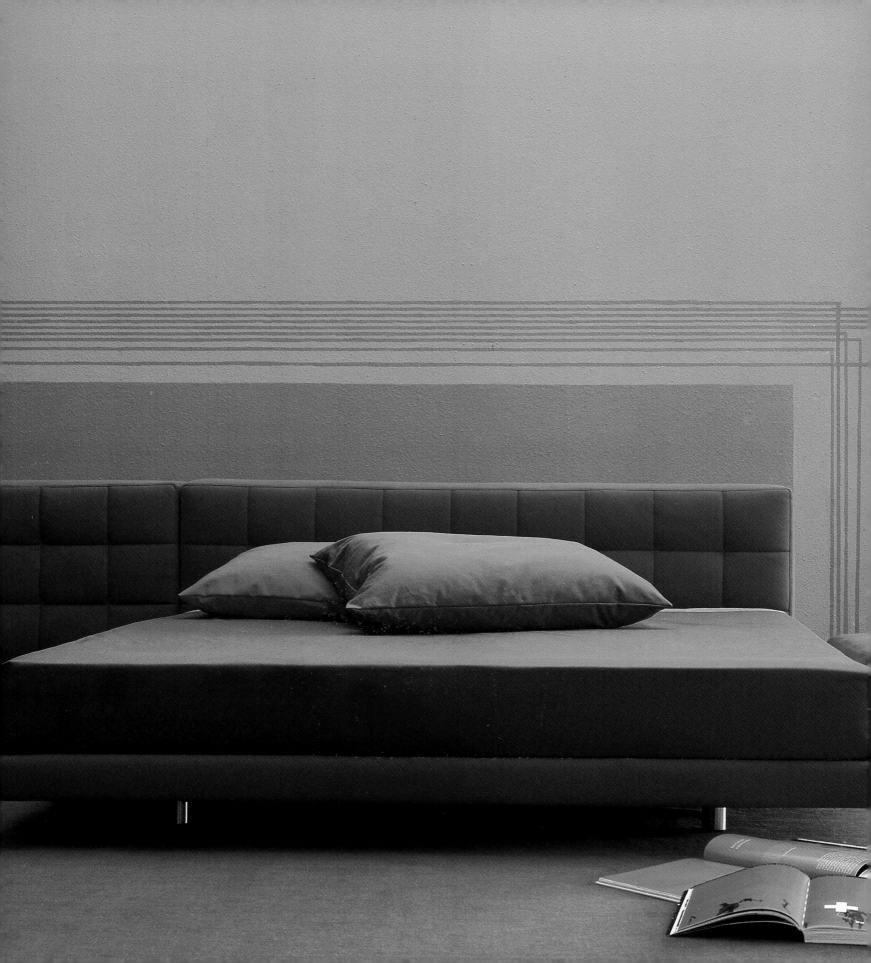

Due to the phenomenon of color temperatures, a red piece of furniture will be perceived as closer than a blue one, even if they are both situated at the same distance. For the same reason, a room with walls painted in a warm color produces a cozy and enveloping sensation, but is visually weightier and makes one feel that the space is smaller. On the contrary, a room with walls painted in a cold color (or one with low intensity or saturation) appears calmer and more spacious, although the atmosphere tends to seem colder. In general, the juxtaposition of cold and warm colors tends to intensify both of them. Color can be used to alter the apparent proportions of a room; if we have a long narrow space, we can give the illusion of better proportions by painting the far wall in a darker color. Similarly, in an excessively square room, we can reduce the effect by painting one of the walls a more intense color than the other three.

Furthermore, both artificial and natural light have a determining effect on the perception of color. For example, the warm light of an incandescent light bulb intensifies yellows and reds, but diminishes the colder colors. Halogen strip lights produce a whiter and brighter light. Fluorescent lights intensify cold colors and diminish warm ones. The orientation of a room determines the quality of the natural light that it receives. Spaces that face north receive less direct light and tend to be colder, while rooms with southern exposure receive warmer light. Generally, in order to balance the color temperature in the room, warm colors are used in rooms that face north while colder colors are used in southern facing ones.

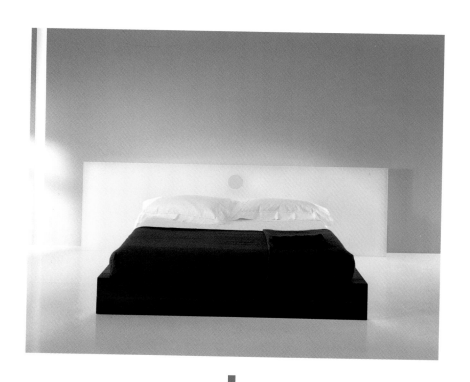

Light and shade show the poetry of form,
just as the folds of a kimono reveal the
hidden positions of the body.

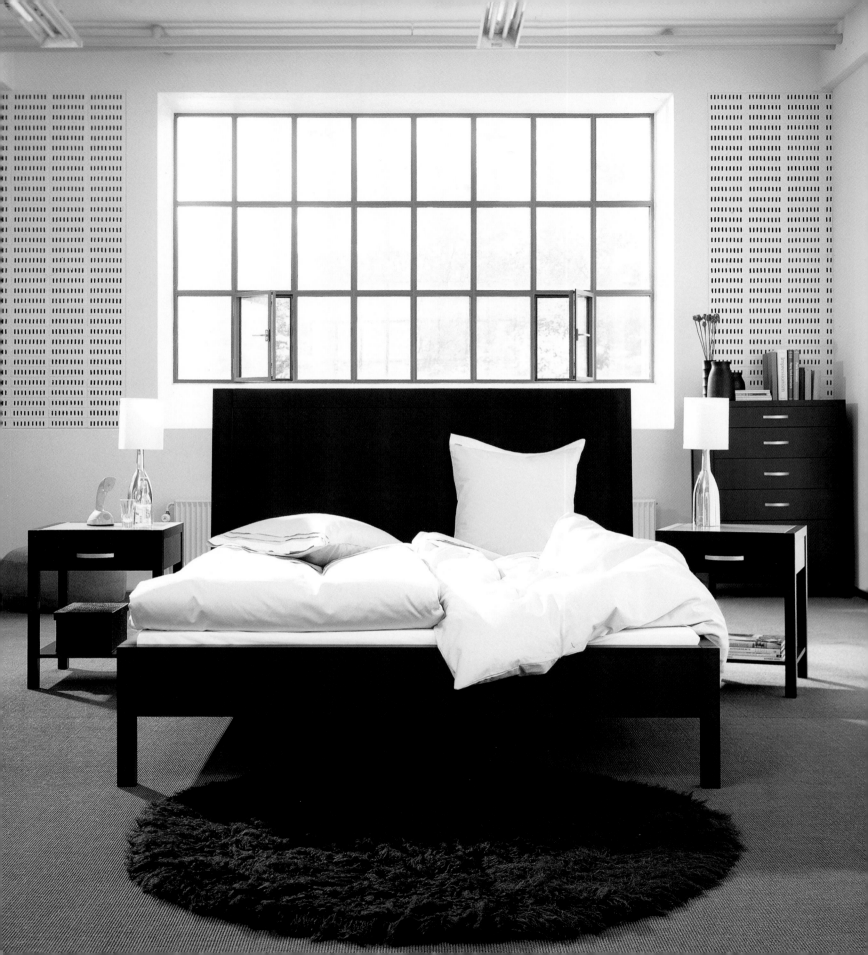

Another variable that influences the perception of color is the relationship between figure and background. The relationship between an object and its environment replies to our tendency to select and order what we see, interpreting any shape as a figure against a background. In fact, there are people that feel disorientated in environments in which the relationship between detail and background is not obvious, for example rooms where the floor, furniture and walls are all of the same color. From this we can deduce that, when we enter a room, we perceive the different shapes that occupy the space based on the differences between their colors. Consequently, we can say that objects are primarily viewed as colors of different shapes and types.

Color & interaction

In order to produce color, a simple base of three pigments is used, which, when mixed together, give a large number of intermediate tones. These are what are known as the **primary colors** (red, yellow and blue), on which all the other colors are based. When we mix two primaries, we obtain **secondary colors**: orange (yellow + red), green (yellow + blue) and violet (red + blue). The combination of a primary color with one of its corresponding secondary colors results in one of the six **tertiary colors**.

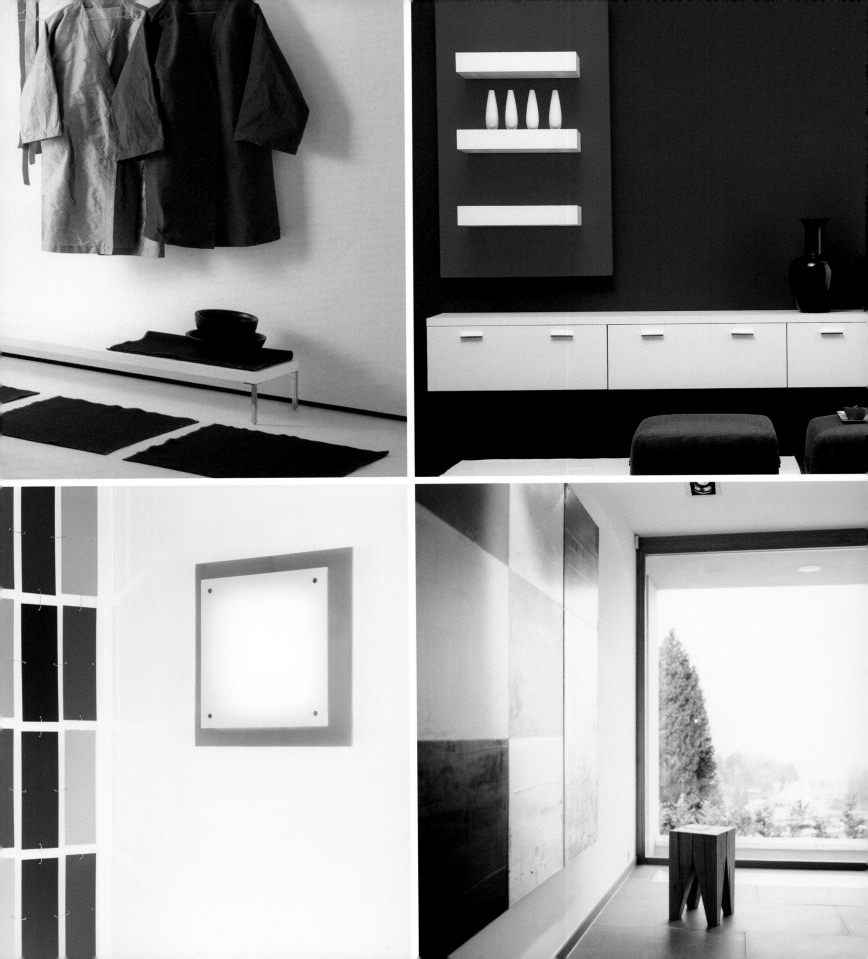

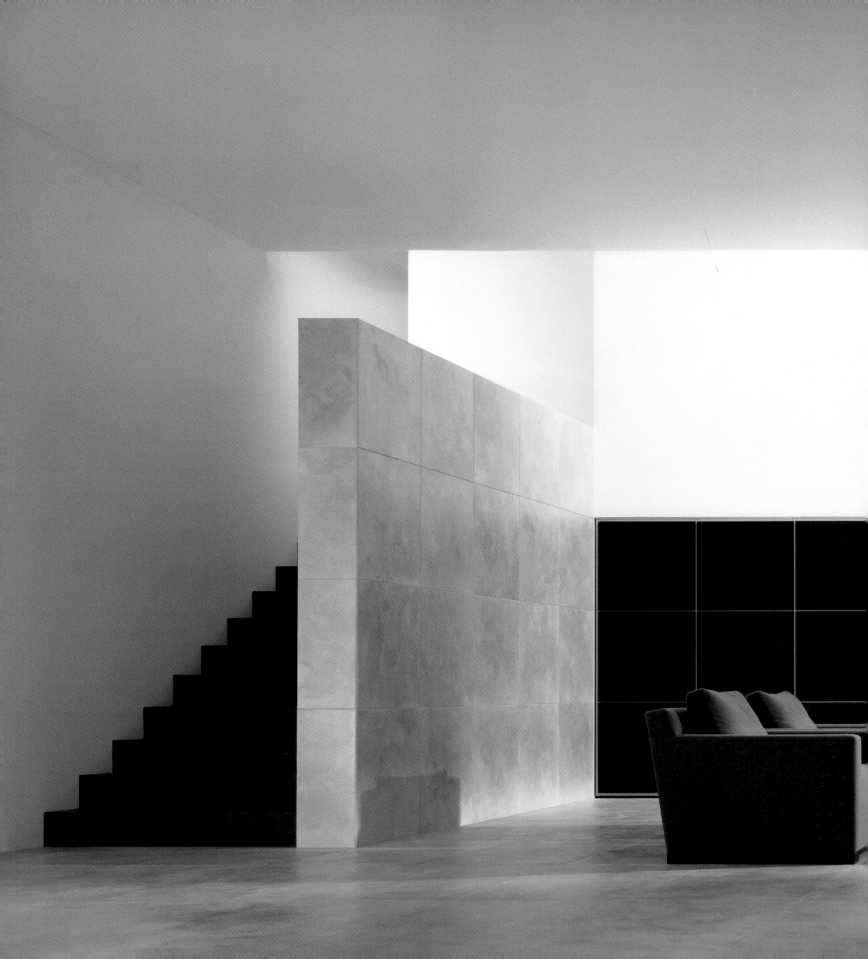

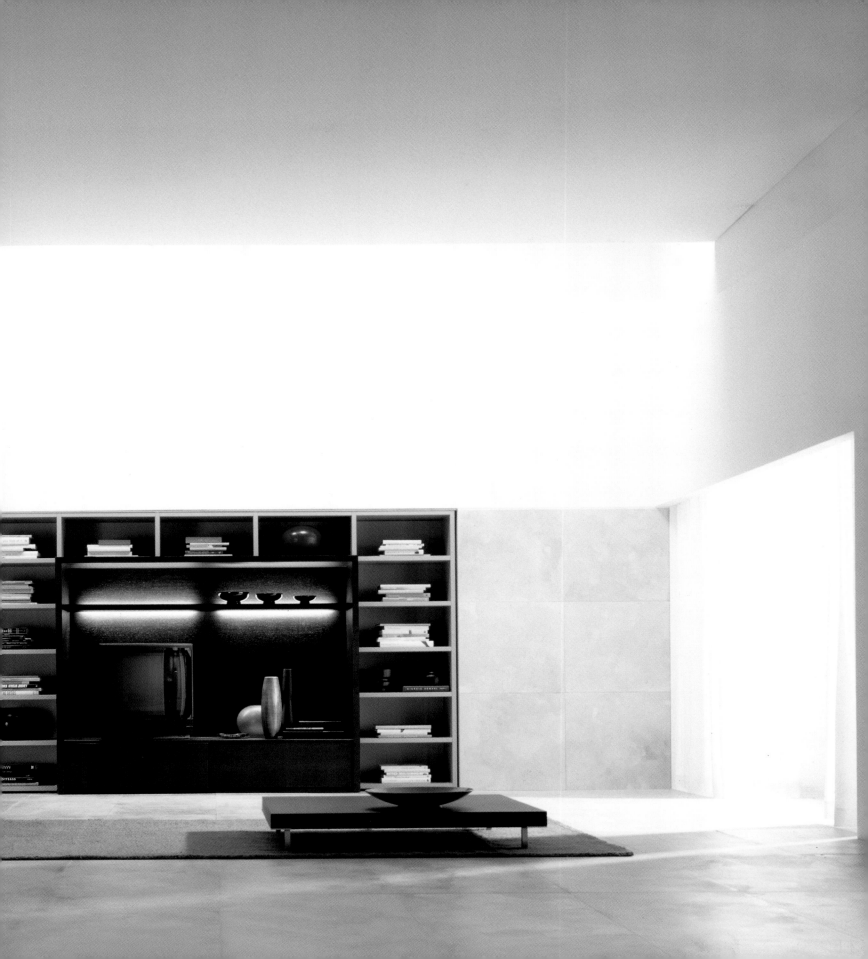

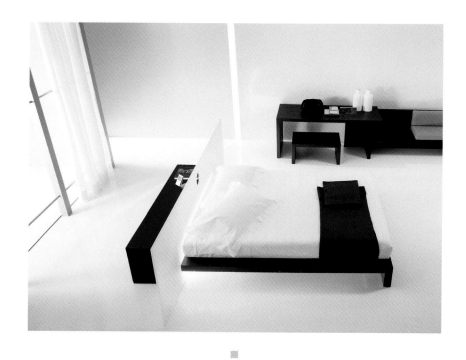

"...to keep on designing furniture, objects and articles for the home, is not the solution to the problems of the house, nor to those of life itself. No embellishment is sufficient to remedy the ravages of time, the errors of man, nor the bestiality of architecture. The solution consists of freeing oneself even more of these design activities, perhaps adopting the technique of a minimum effort in a general process of reduction."

Superstudio design group.

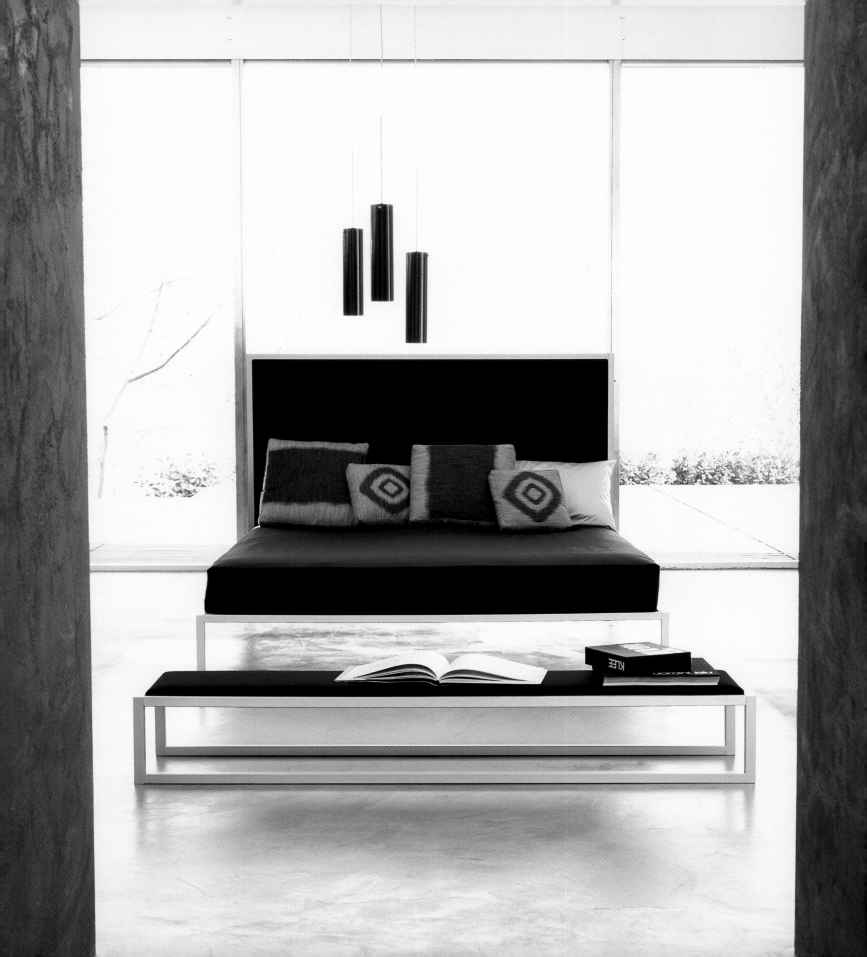

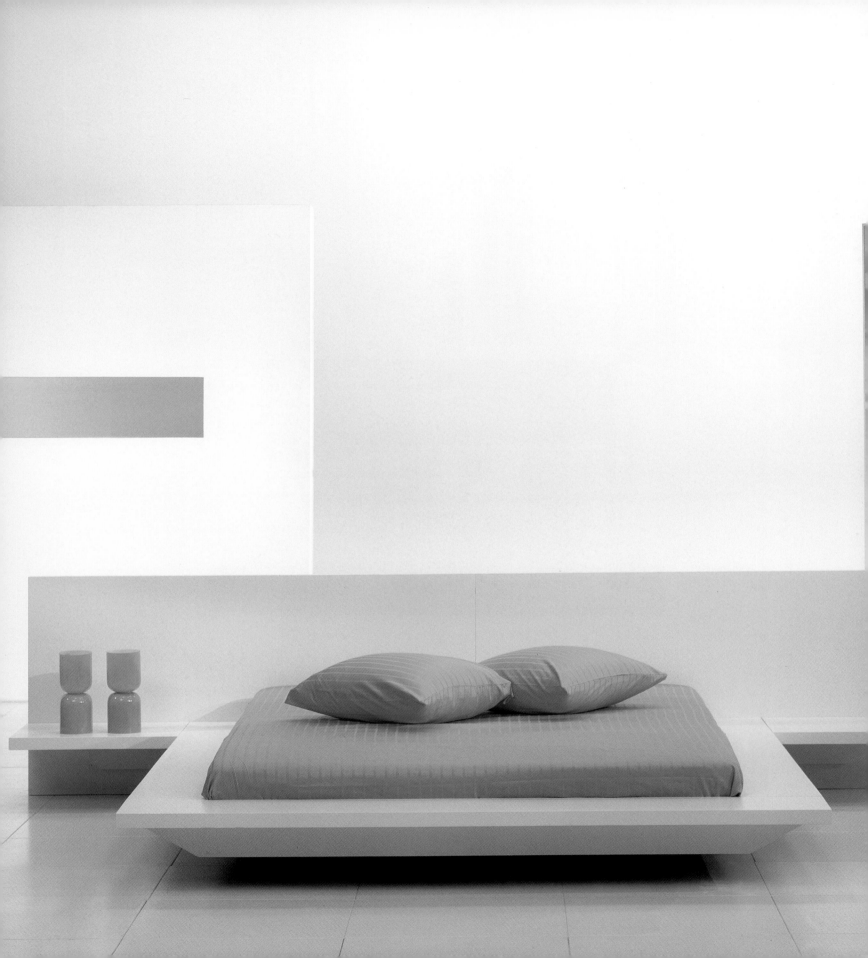

Colors are defined by three metric variables. These allow us to order them by creating an identification system for the multiple chromatic variations possible: **tone, value** and **saturation**. The *tone or shade* is the qualitative variation of the color, and depends on the wavelength of its radiation; the human eye is capable of distinguishing 12.000 tones. Colors without tone are called achromatic or neutral colors, and are white, black and neutral grays. The *value* or *luminosity* is the quantity of light that a color reflects; white is the color that has the highest value. Each color has different degrees of luminosity. The *saturation* or *intensity* is the degree to which a tone predominates. Consequently, a pale color has little saturation while the primary colors are saturated to the max; the saturation can be varied by adding black or white so that the color appears brighter or duller.

The **chromatic circle** is a visual system for ordering colors that takes the primary colors and their binary combinations as its base. This is particularly useful for decoration because it helps us to understand the relationships that exist between colors. Based on this, we can create color schemes that are betteadapted to each individual. In the circle, the complementary color of each tone is directly opposite it.

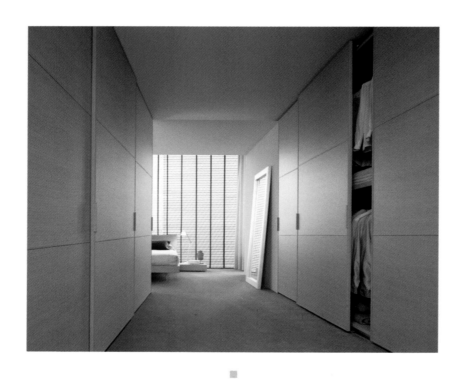

"Their mass does not take
up any space."

Marcel Breuer,
describing his steel tube chairs

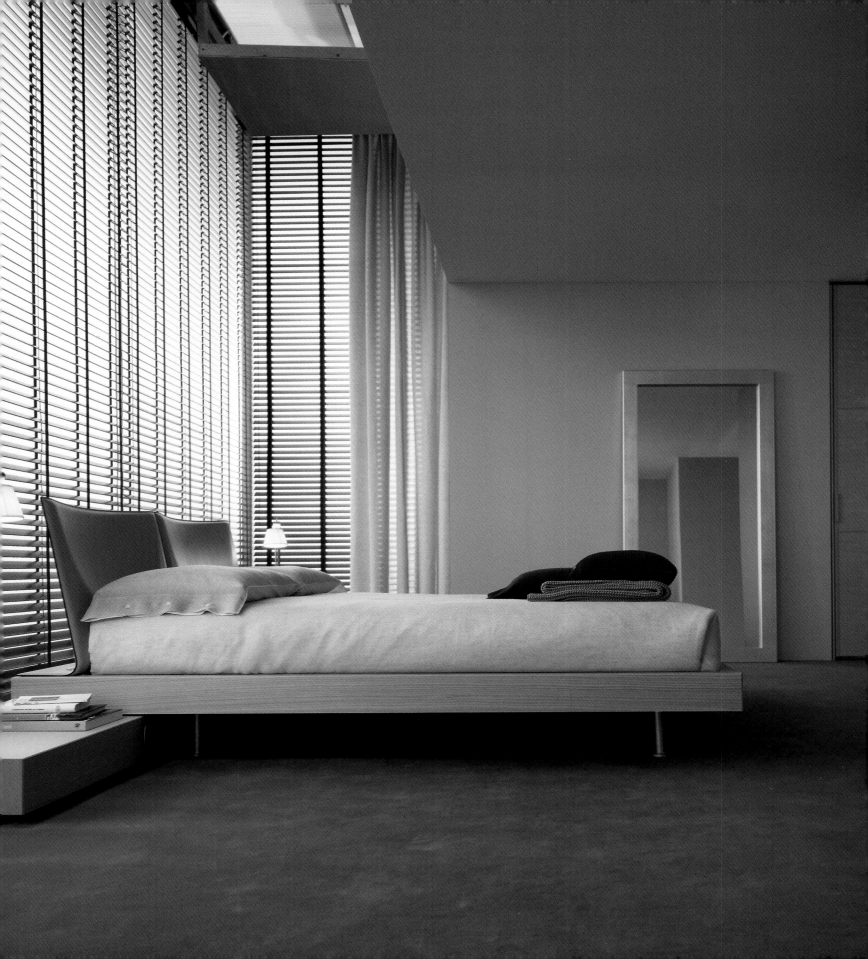

Chromatic relationships demonstrate that the perception of a tone is relative and depends on its relationship with the environment and other tones, which can significantly alter the appearance of the tones involved. In this comparison, the variables of tone, value and saturation are very important. With the chromatic circle, we can see that the most distinct tones are the complementary ones, between which there is a maximum degree of contrast that accentuates their differences. If, on the other hand, the tones are not significantly different, there is a affinity between them.

We can base our decorative criteria on different types of **color combinations** in order to create harmonious atmospheres that are pleasing to the eye and show an intrinsic sense of order positioned on the midpoint between boredom and chaos. Although there are no fixed rules because harmony is the result of experimentation and a matter of personal taste, the main color combinations are: monochromatic, based on value and saturation variations of a single color; analogous, which combine colors close to each other on the color wheel; and complementary, which are created from colors in opposing positions on the color wheel.

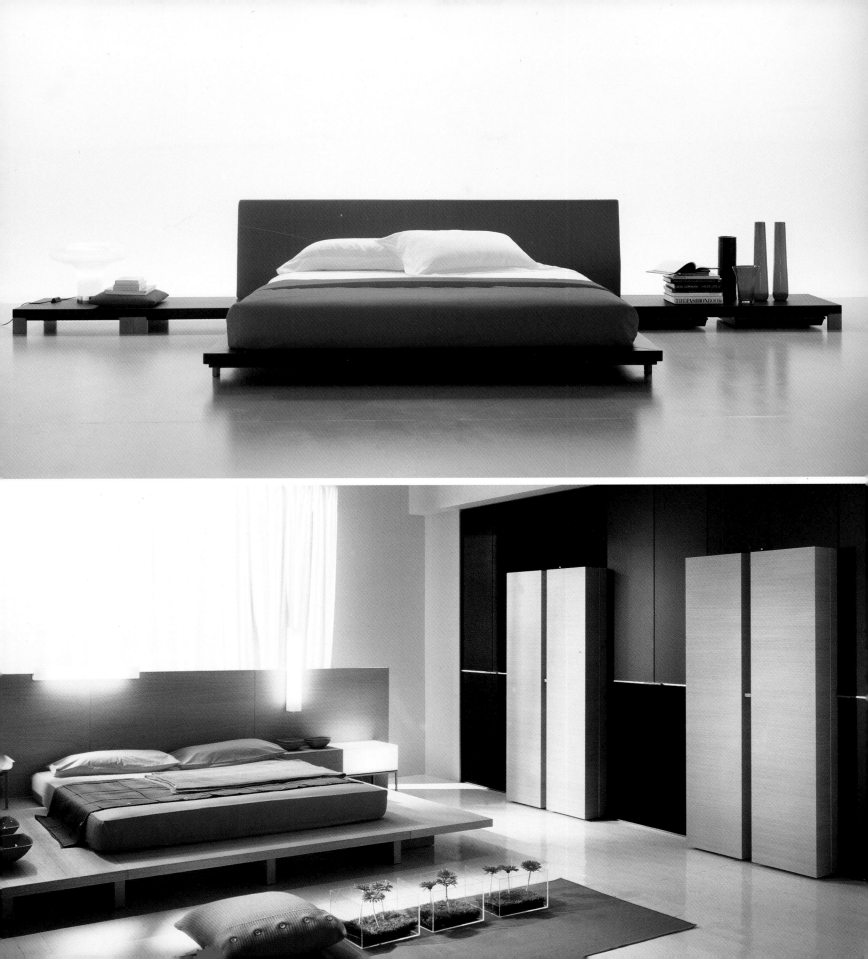

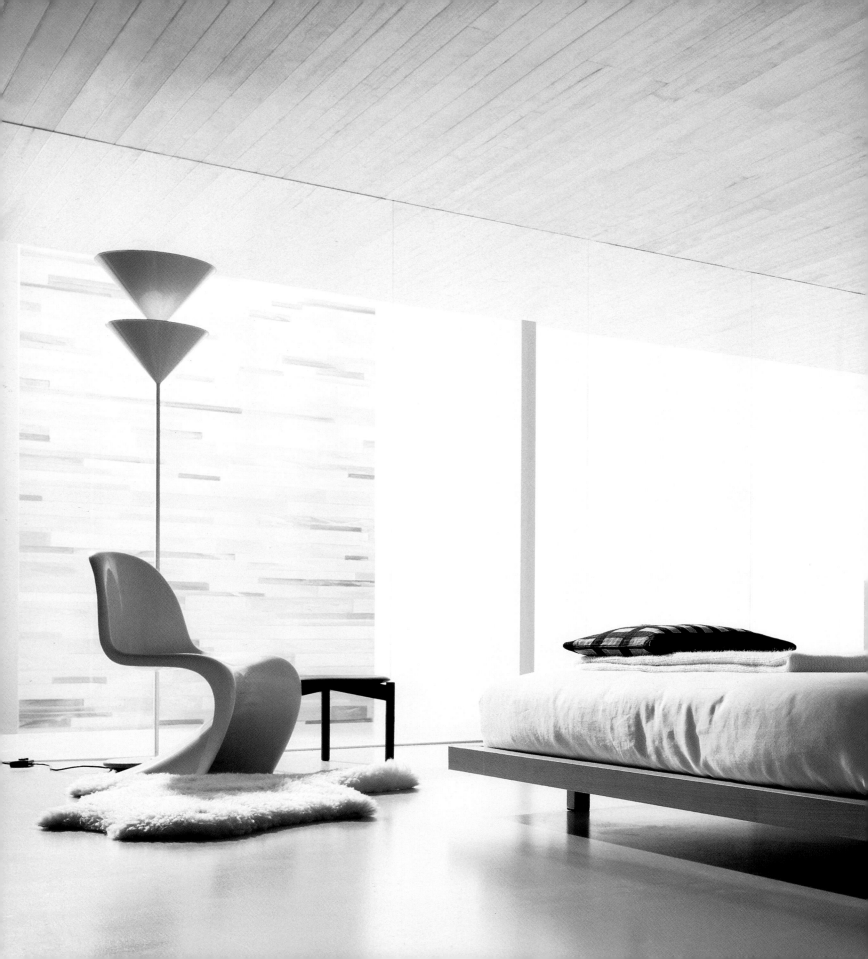

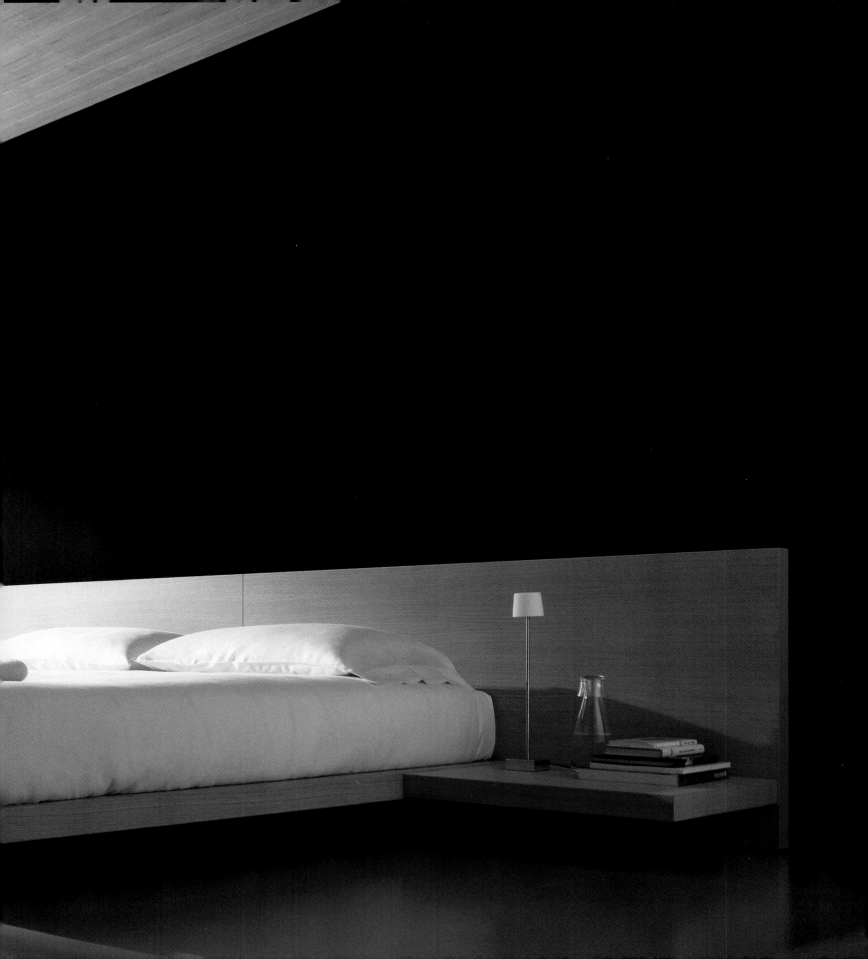

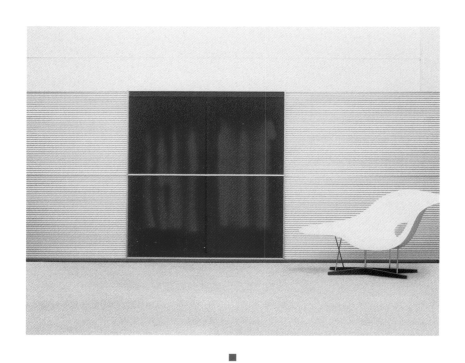

■

"Pieces of furniture are not dead
objects, because they influence you in
subtle ways. Their particular qualities or
weaknesses will make you for your whole
life: they will enlarge you or shrink you,
they will reward you or punish you,
in a definitive way."

Leon Krier

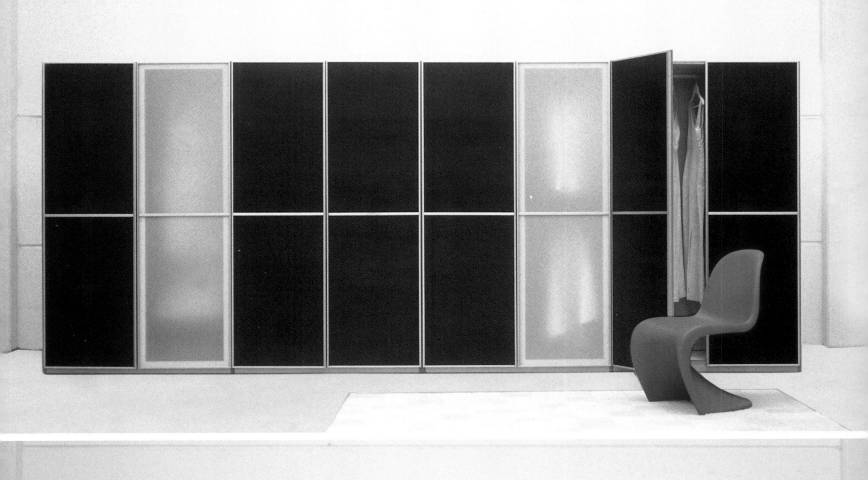

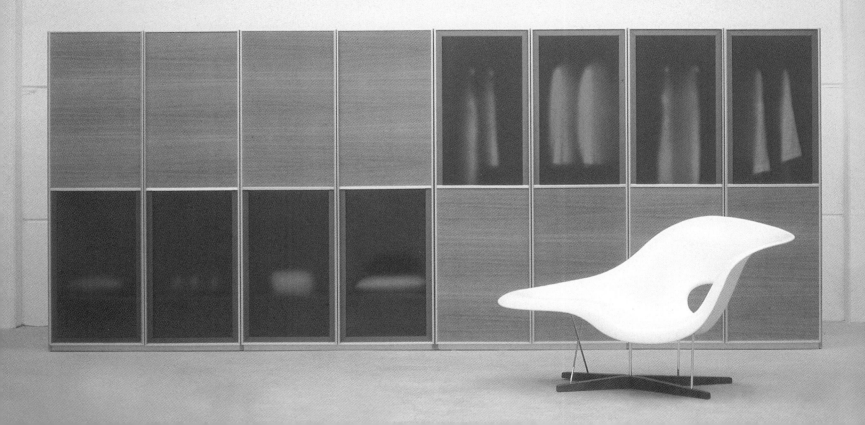

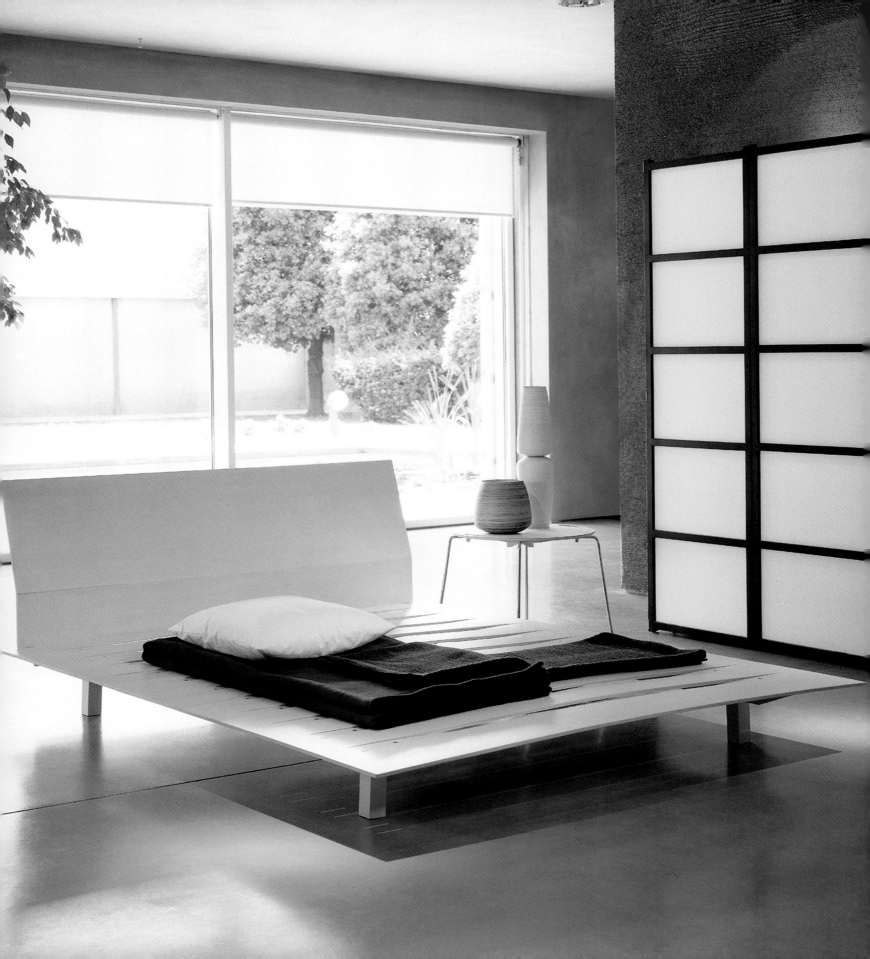

Color & Psychology

The color that we perceive around us not only provides us with objective information about the world, but also affects our sentiments and our emotional state. Reciprocally, the perception of color is also affected by the influence of psychological and social factors, because we react to color differently depending on who we are and what concrete significance our culture gives to the different colors. For this reason, the symbolic appearance of a color may have very different connotations depending on the period or culture. In reality, giving meanings to colors is a tradition that is as old as humanity; for example, purple in the Roman Empire, blue in eighteen century Europe and yellow in Imperial China are color variants attributed to royalty in different eras and cultures.

Humanity's need to develop color symbolism is directly related to its need to experience the well-being that is produced by color perception. In this sense, some believe that the human capacity to feel color derives from our desire to obtain pleasure and from our need for survival.

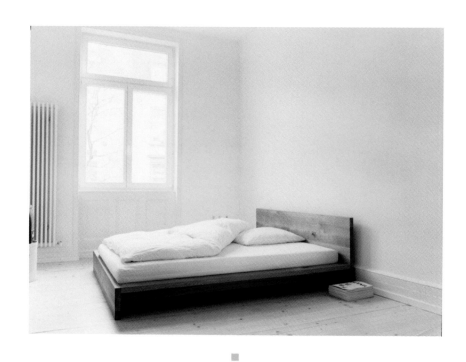

Frank Lloyd Wright conceived a building
as a complete creation, where the
interior furniture should be in harmony
with the shape and materials
of the structure, created to be a
part of a specific
geographic location.

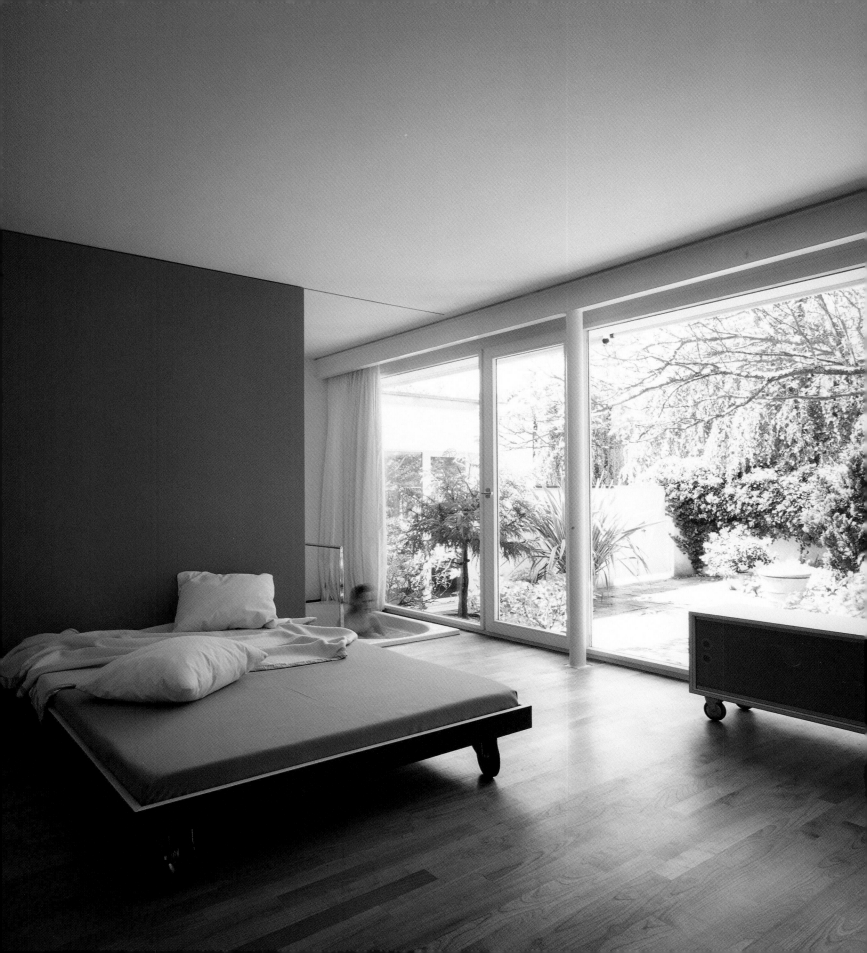

Goethe once said, "Colors act upon the soul. They can stimulate sensations, awaken emotions and ideas that calm us or excite us and provoke sadness or happiness." Said differently, color plays a fundamental role in the world in which we live and, consequently, in our lives as far as its capacity to alter our emotions and provoke reactions and sensations. Color can animate or depress, stimulate or tranquilize, unify or divide, make larger or smaller, invite conversation or disagreement, provoke interest or confusion, and it can contribute to the image we have of ourselves and those around us. For this reason, the choice of color in the decoration of our homes should not be taken arbitrarily, but should be done considering this series of conditioning elements.

In general terms, that could be stated differently in terms of the many studies that have examined the psychological effects of colors, each of the colors of the spectrum are associated with determined **emotional effects,** which can be useful when choosing the color of a wall or a piece of furniture.

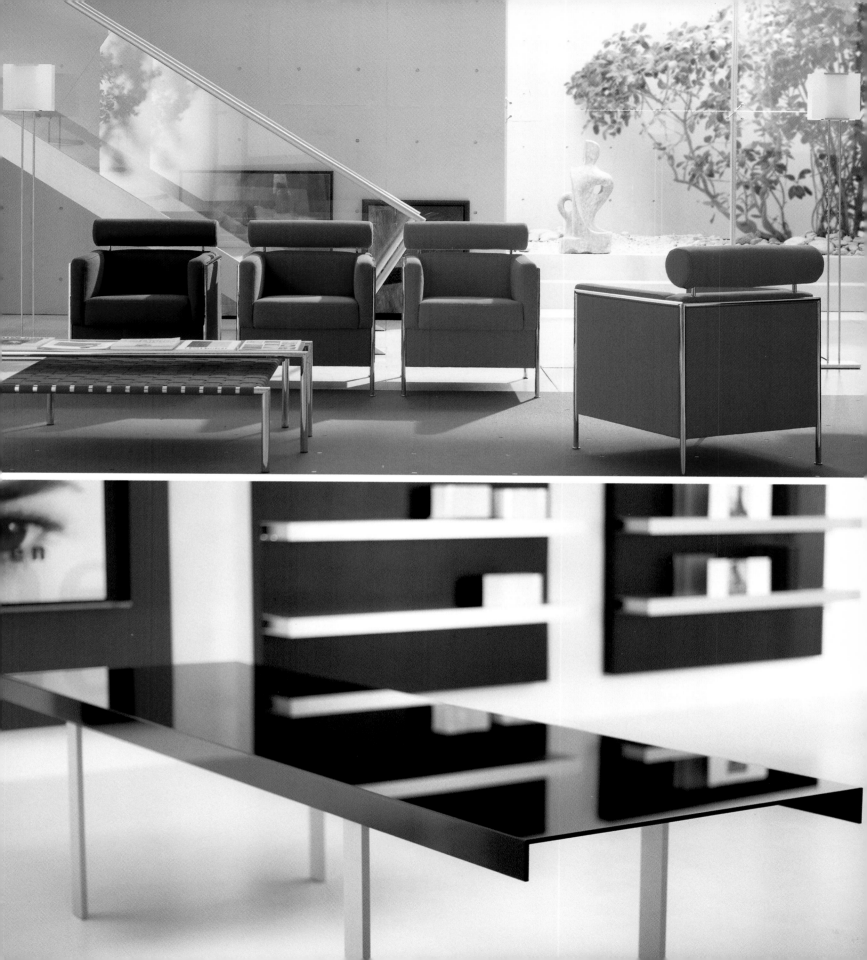

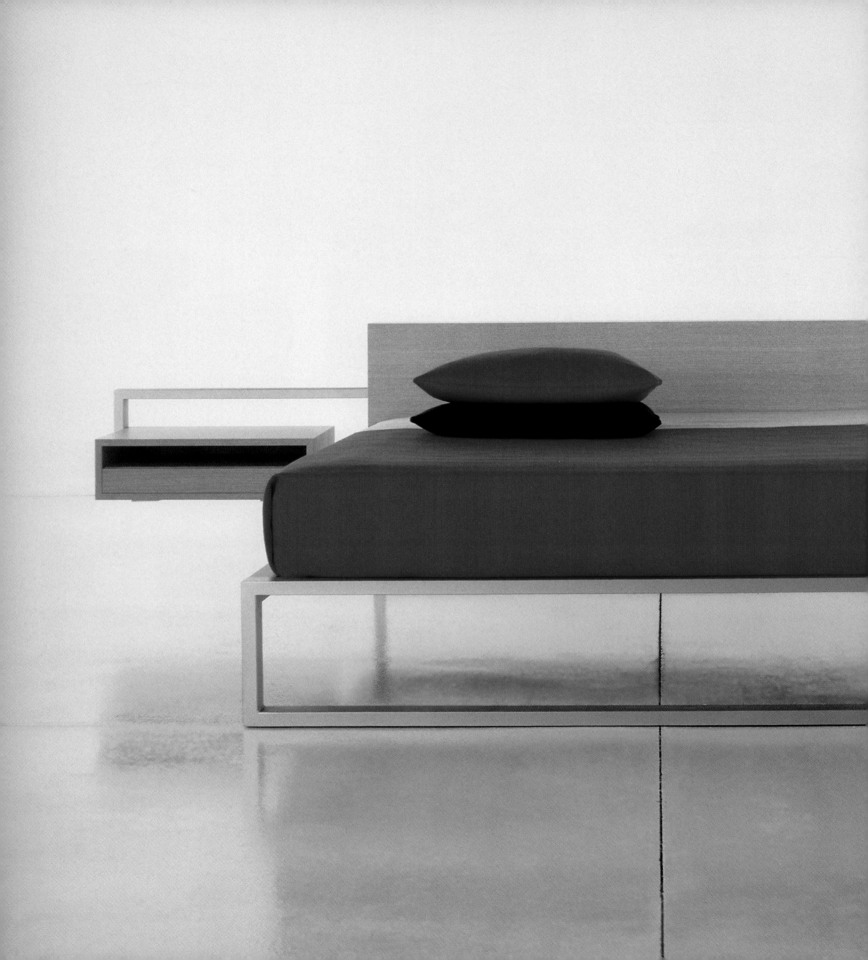

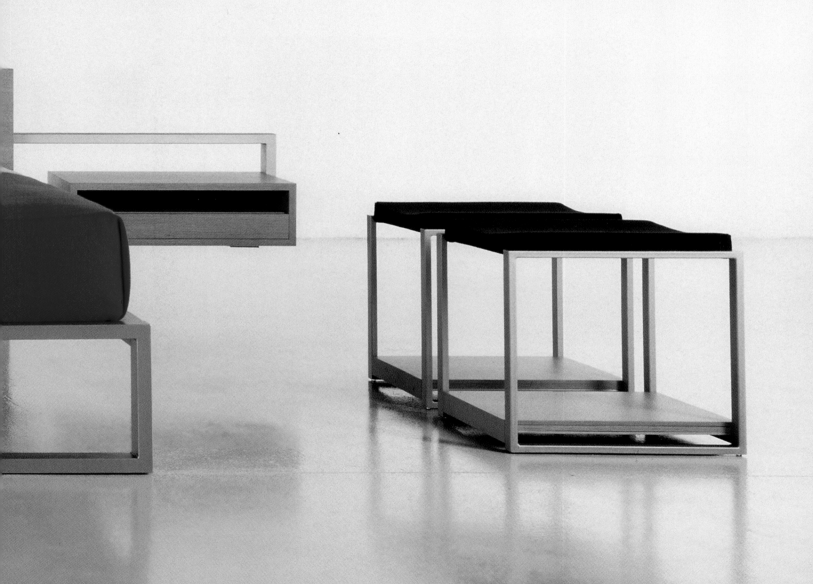

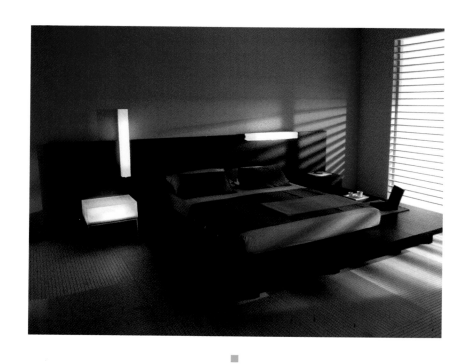

Observing the effects that colors have
on each other is the starting point for
understanding the relativity of color.

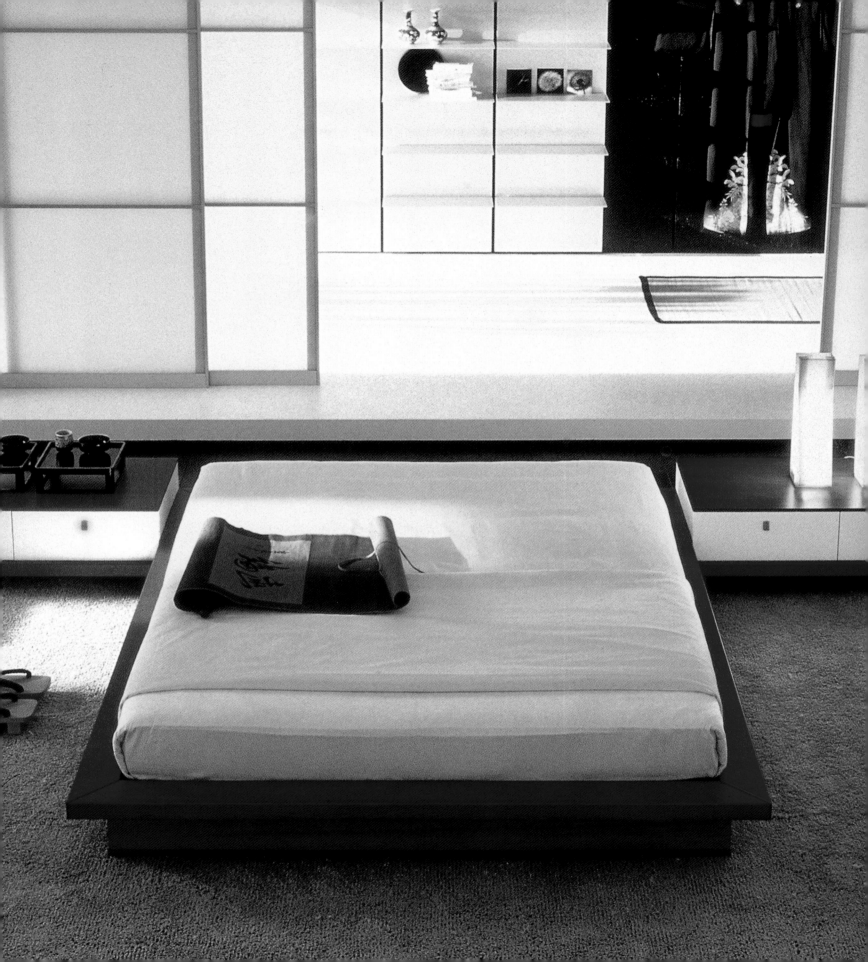

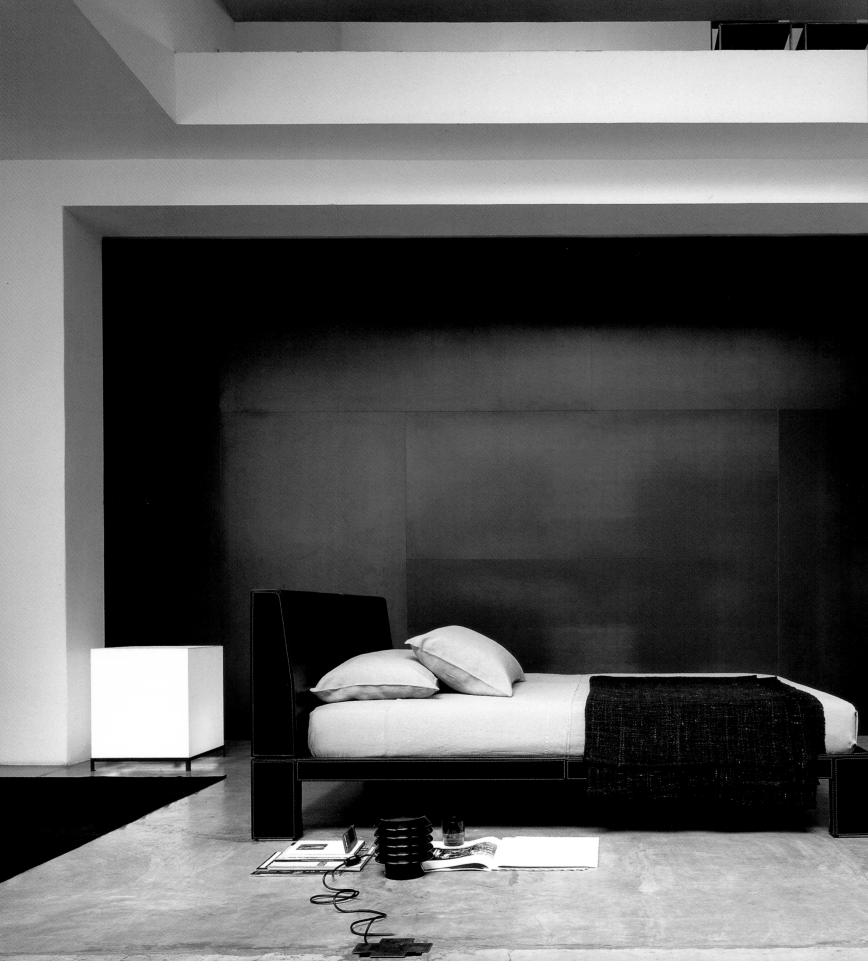

RED: Reddish tones generate a sensation of heat and tend to move closer to the observer due to the fact that they have a longer wavelength and consequently, a shorter focal point. On a symbolic level, red is associated with happiness and contentment, along with the heart, flesh, emotion and passion. An intense red is exciting and is the color that makes the greatest emotional impact. When it tends towards pink, it becomes more relaxed, more friendly and more feminine. In decoration, bright red combines perfectly with neutral colors such as white or black that accentuate its expressive strength even more, or with brownish tones.

ORANGE: In the words of Wassily Kandinsky, "Orange is red brought closer to humanity by yellow." It is an unmistakably warm color, closely associated with autumn and the earth. It is stimulating, spiritually optimistic and generates energy and happiness. Psychologically, orange behaves in the same way as yellow: it is animated, expansive, rich and extroverted. It is a color that is particularly oriented towards food and for this reason it is often used in kitchens.

YELLOW: This color is traditionally associated with intelligence. The color of spring, the sun, light, intensity, happiness, with the ability to stimulate and animate, in its purest form it radiates heat and inspiration. Yellow is frequently used in children's rooms; in China, it has been venerated as a favorable color since time immemorial.

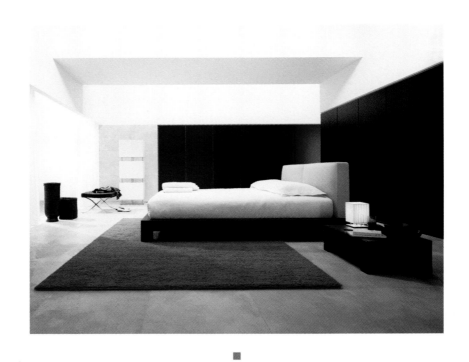

Shubui, a fundamental part of the Zen
philosophy, involves, the strengthening of
self-discipline and the casting out of
everything which is not essential.

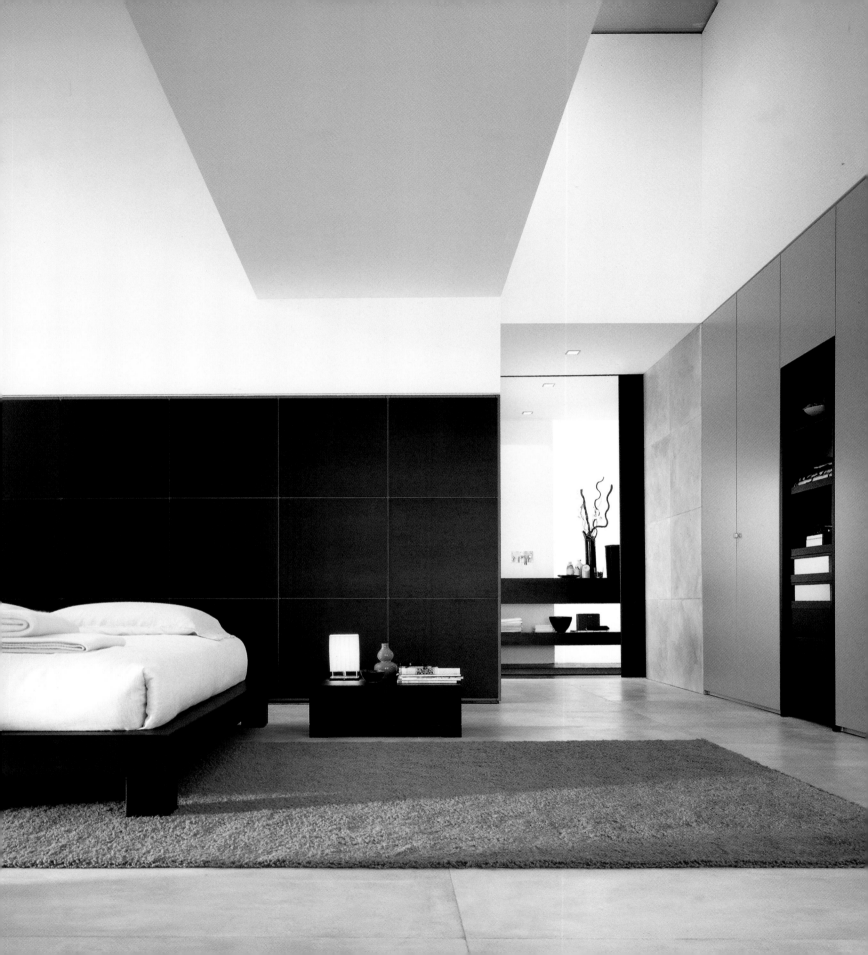

GREEN: The color of life and of the silent power of nature; green's attributes include a relaxing effect and sedative properties and it is related to the qualities of stability, security and emotional balance. It is one of the most ambivalent colors of the spectrum and the one with the most opposing meanings: it is associated both with envy and with love, because is the color of Venus. There is an ancient belief that it has beneficial relaxing effects on the eyes.

BLUE: The color of the spirit, of the sky and of water; blue is related to characteristics of nobility. It has been classified as a cold color and, in contrast to warm colors, it gives the sensation of distance owing to the fact that its wavelength is shorter and this increases its focal point, making it appear further away. Although it is fundamentally a healthy color, at times, it can signify melancholy or sadness. It is especially recommended for bedrooms or places of rest.

VIOLET: Born out of the union of opposite, violet absorbs the passion of red and the spirituality of blue. This contrast generates tonalities that can provoke both desire and aversion (this is what is known as "psychologically oscilating" tonality). Thus, combined with skill it evokes celestial delicacy or great richness but, if combined clumsily, gives a sense of decomposition. Violet is related to intimacy and sublimation and indicates profound sentiments. Violet light possesses the most energy and it was not in vain that Claude Monet said "... finally, I have found the true color of the atmosphere, it is violet. Fresh air is violet".

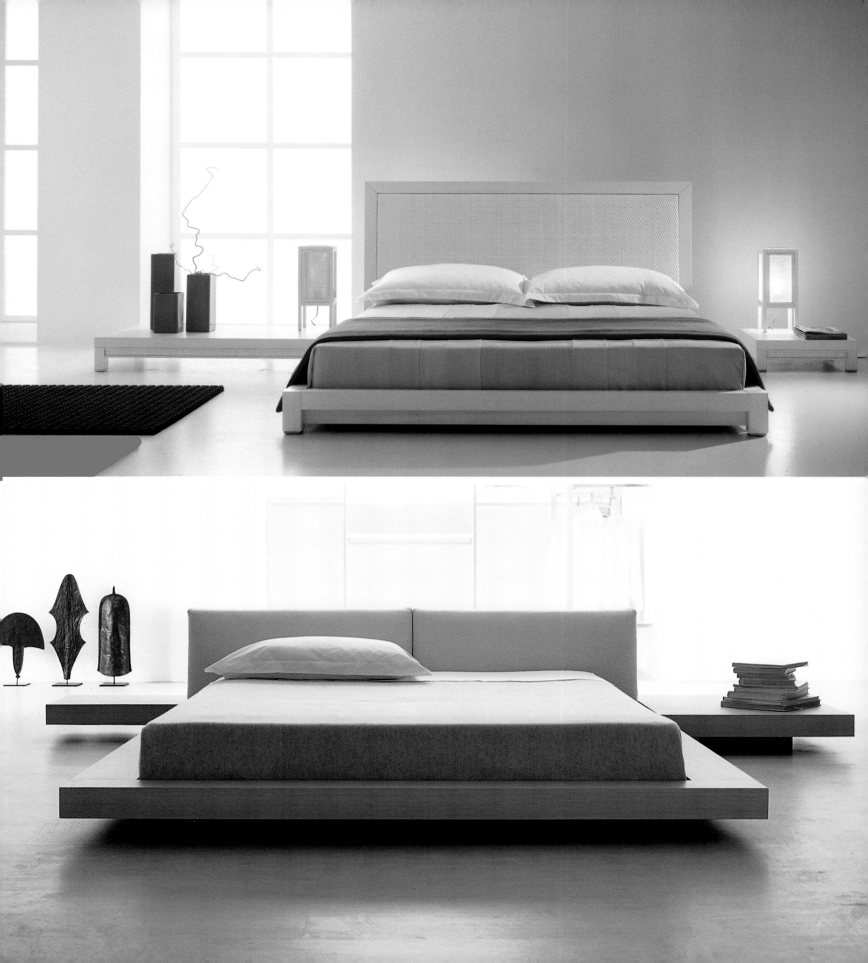

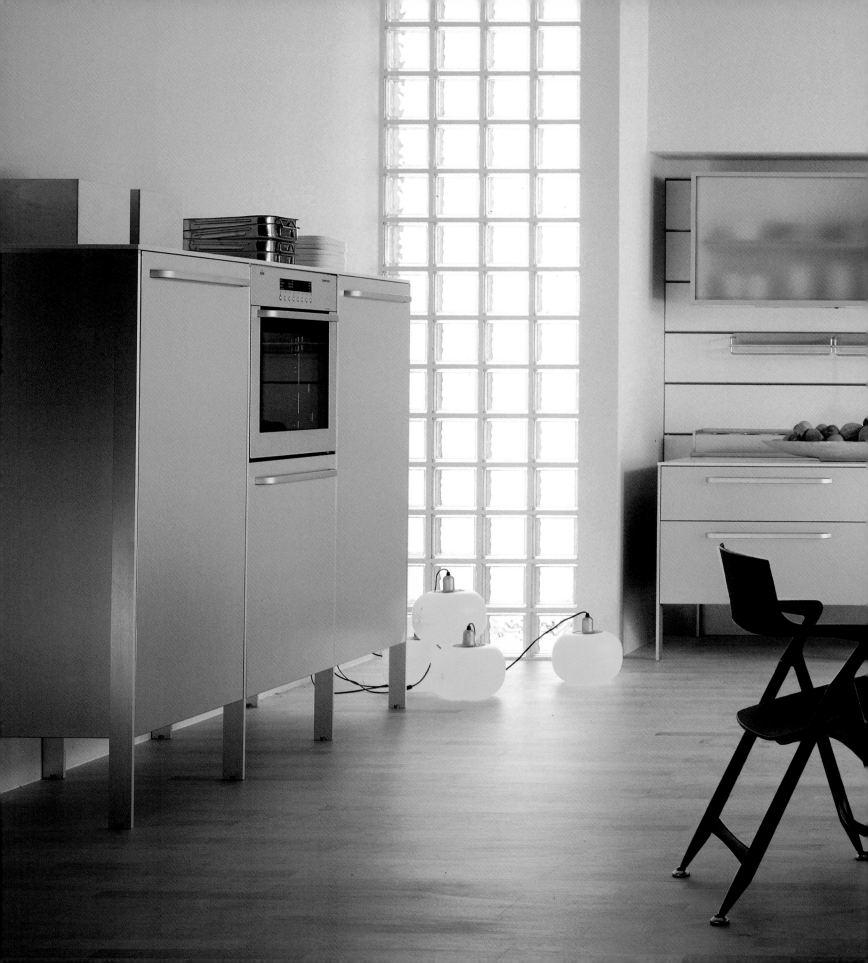

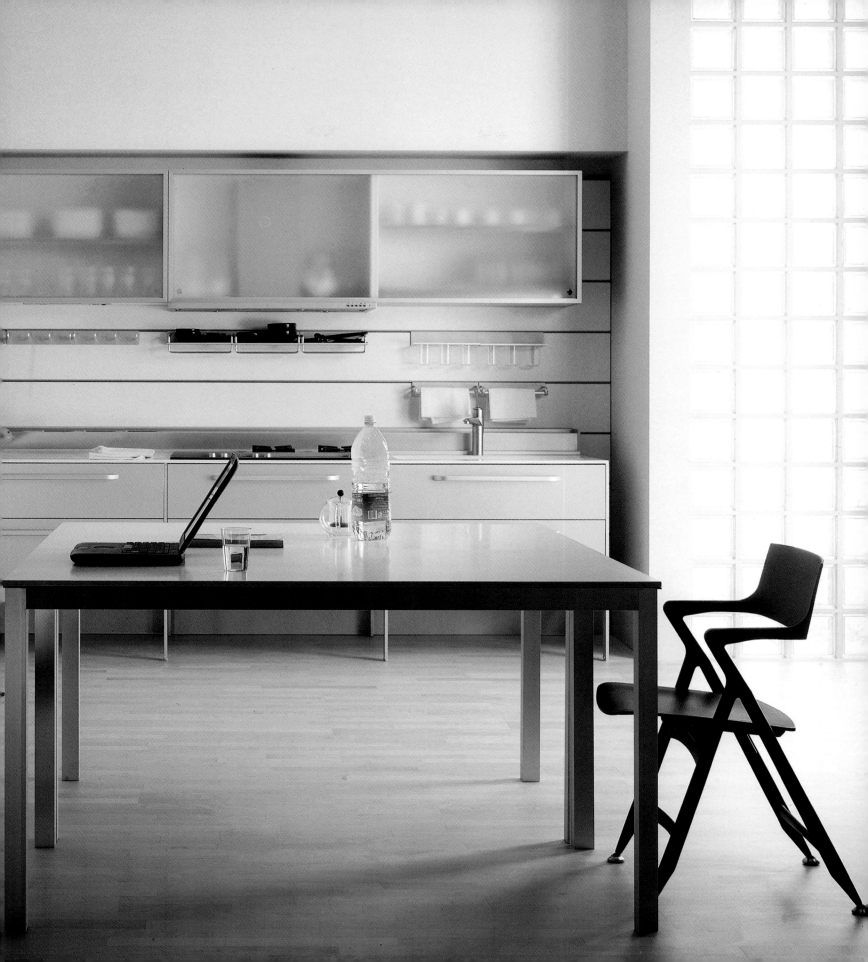

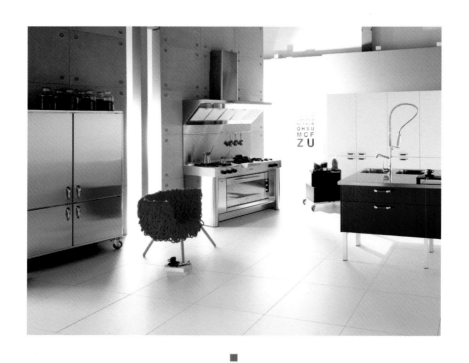

The ornament has no place in the Zen
tradition, because it comes from
the superficial and ostentatious
part of our minds.

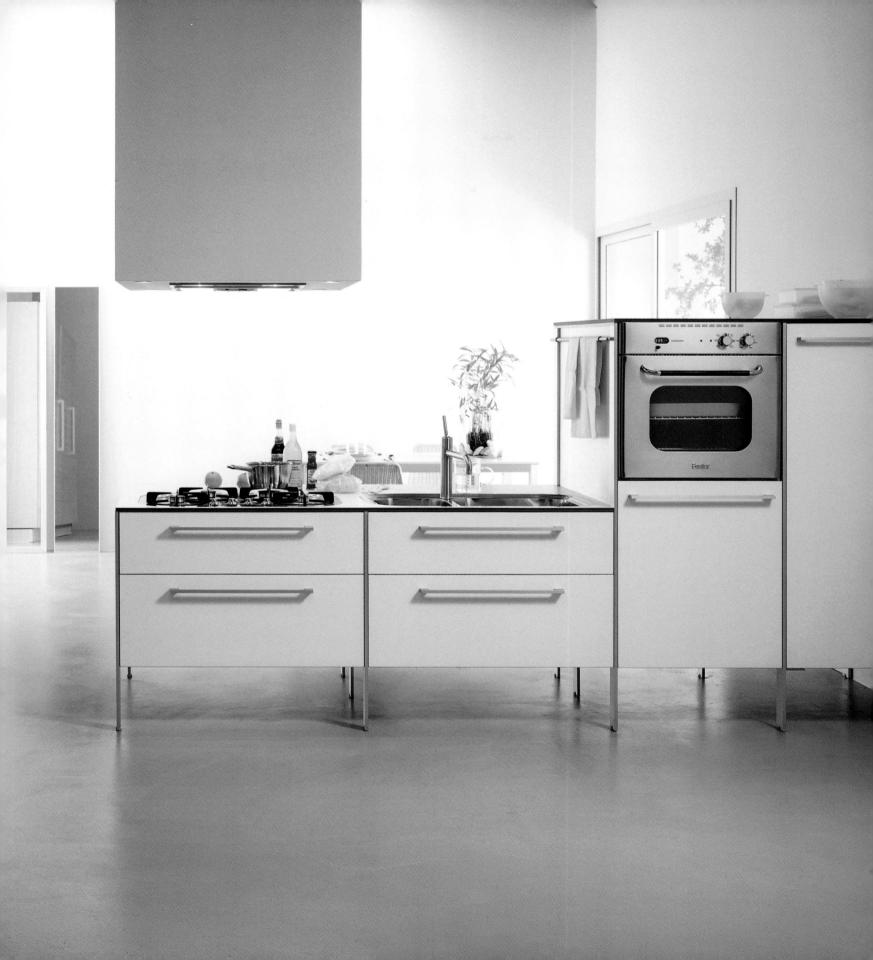

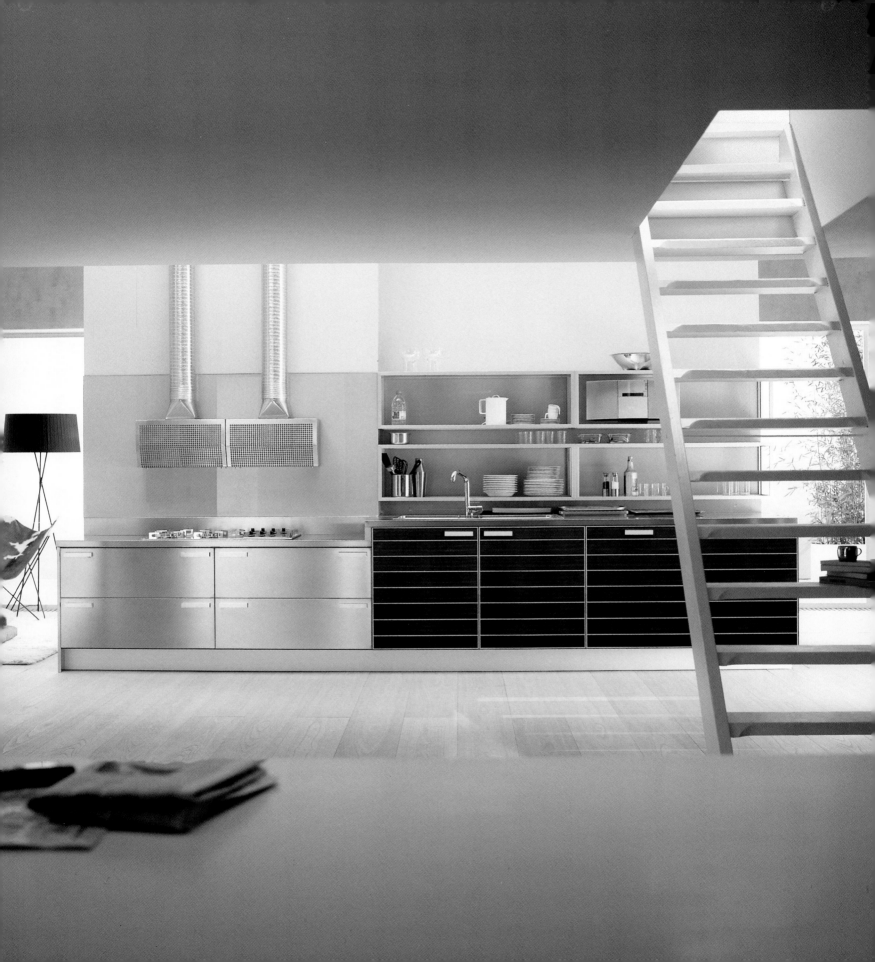

Minimalism & Color: Expressive Simplicity

Bearing in mind everything that has been covered so far, what does living in an environment built on the principles of minimalism, and on those of perception and the psychology of color, mean? Primarily, answers some of the needs posed by today's society in industrialized countries. Secondarily, in relation to mankind's needs in particular, it means going beyond the strict and more austere minimalist approaches that were prevalent in interior design in the nineties.

As far as an answer to the needs of society, minimalism presents itself as a philosophy of life that preaches a lifestyle based on simplicity, rejecting the uncontrolled consumerism imposed by the media. Applied on a sound basis, that is to say, as an answer to an internal need, and not as another fashion or stylistic trend, the creation of a vital environment based on simplicity could be qualified as a revolution and a liberation.

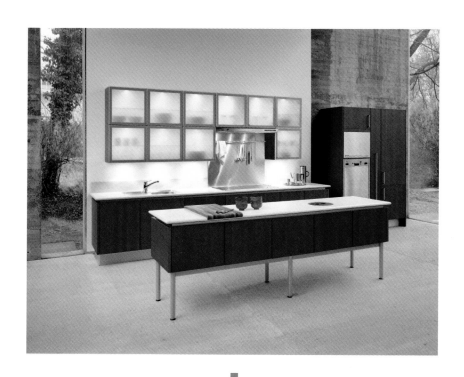

"People are the measurement
for all furniture."

Friedrich Wilhelm Möller

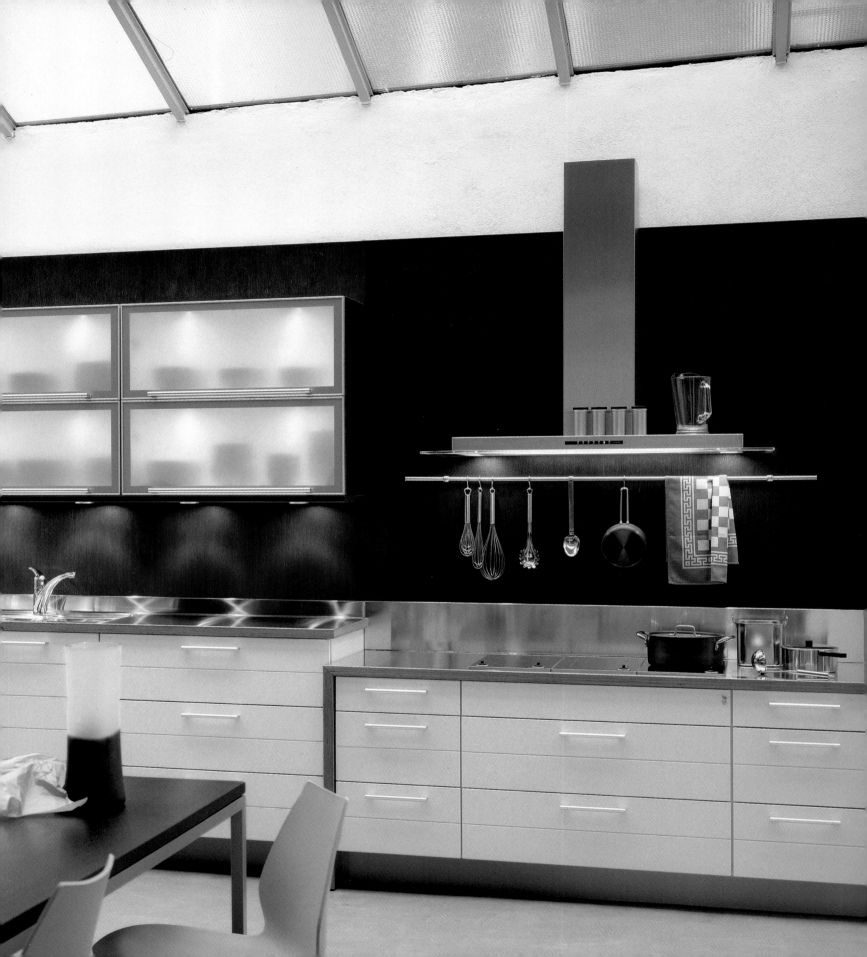

Speaking in general terms, minimalism in decoration could be defined as a look towards the spontaneity of the present, as a free moment, without historical burdens and worries about the future. The important thing, as highlighted by the postulates of the artistic movement and *Zen Buddhism*, is the immediate experience of the here and now. The goal is the naked beauty of the moment, which finds maximum expressiveness in the least ornamentation possible. In fact, it is a complex process of liberating everything superfluous, a reaction to the current trend for accumulating unnecessary things which rapidly become obsolete. Minimalism is a return to authenticity, to the intrinsic quality of materials and textures, as opposed to the superficiality of useless objects.

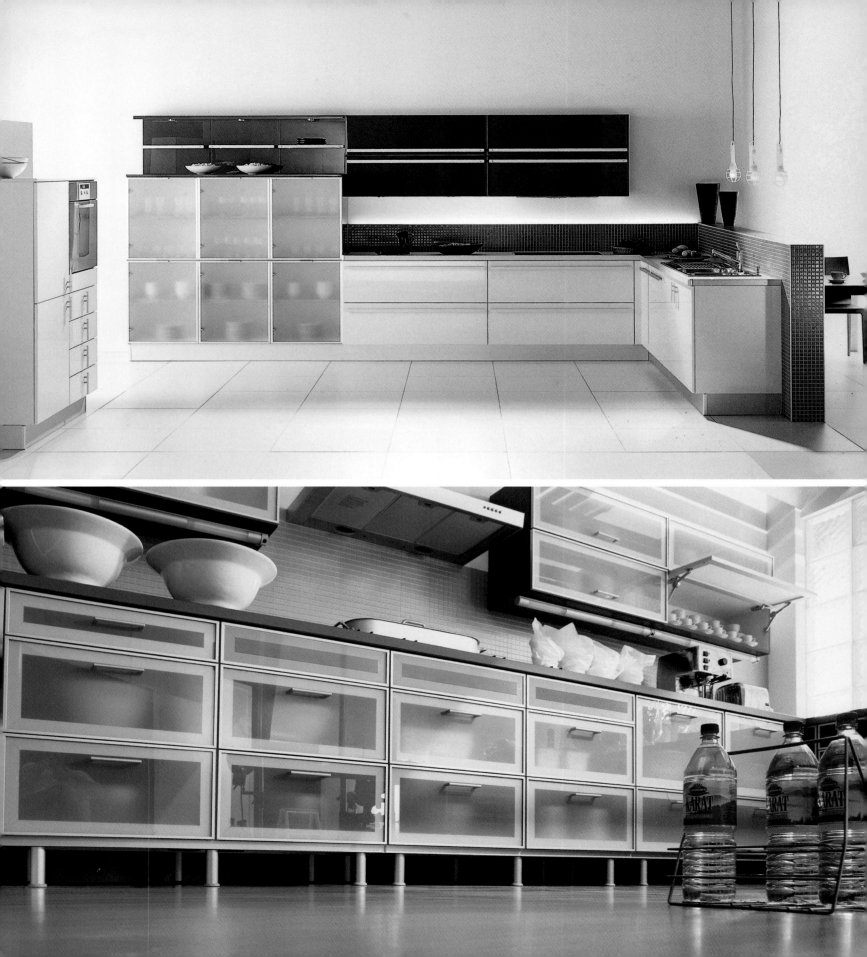

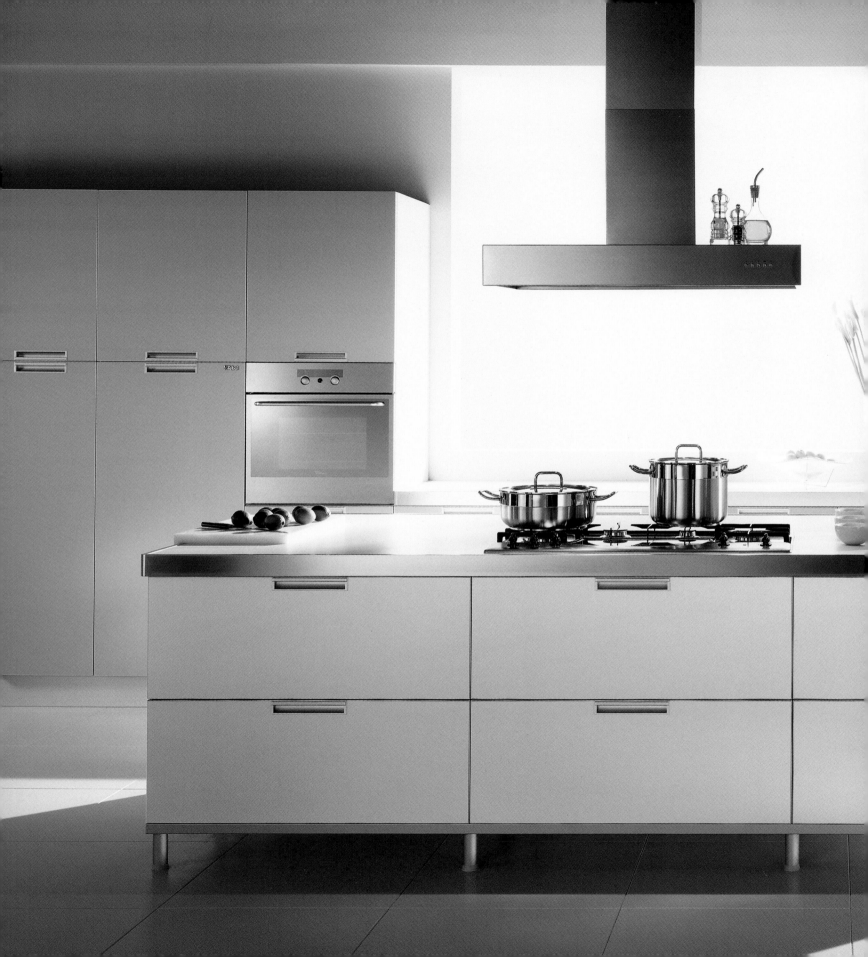

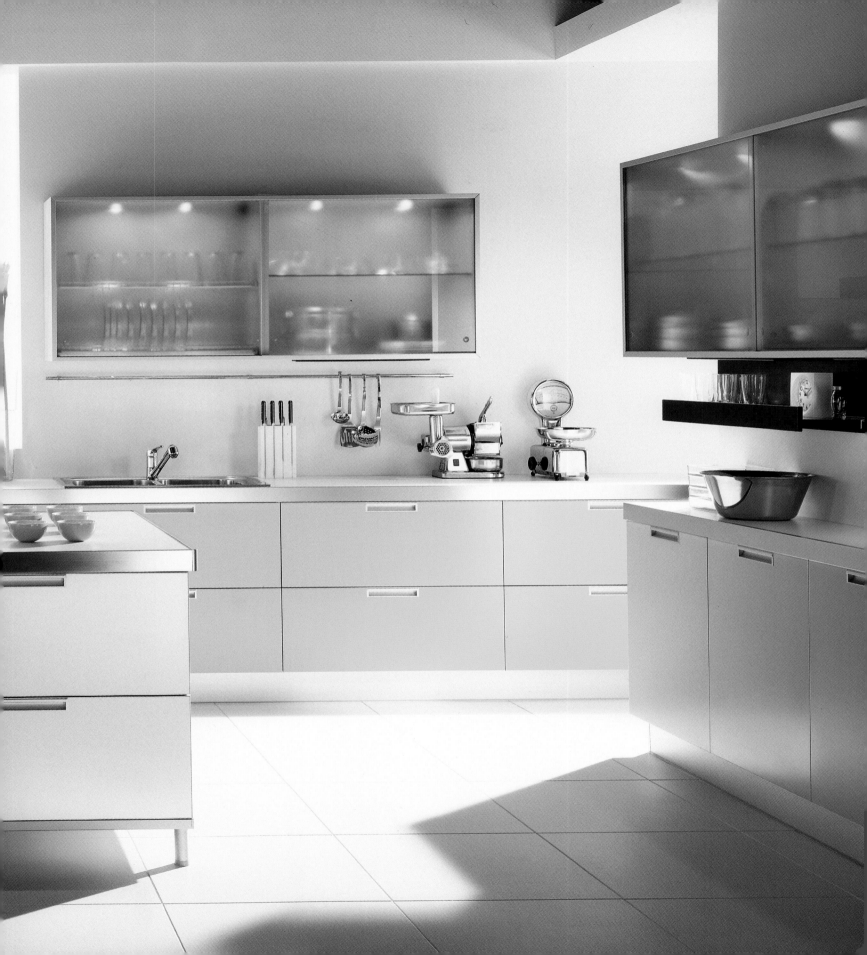

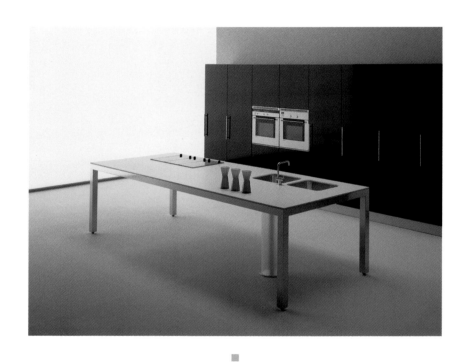

The industrial concept of maximum
functionality drives the design of
minimalist kitchens, which seem to
gravitate around a nucleus, usually
tinted with color.

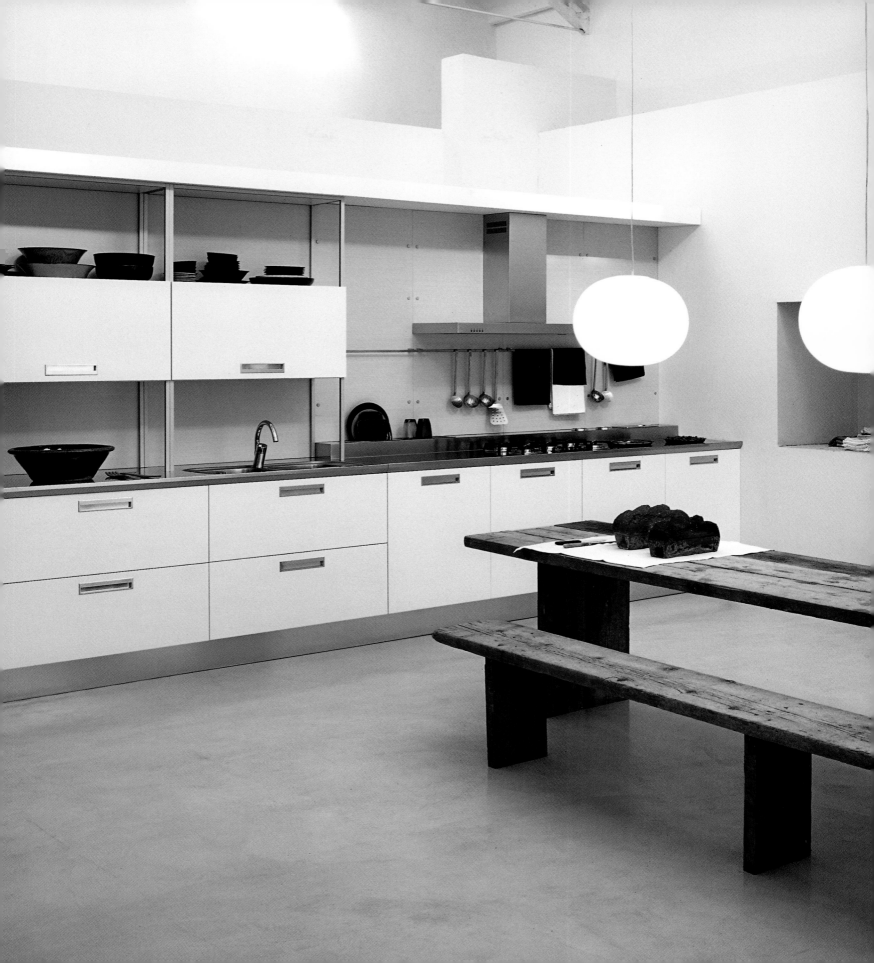

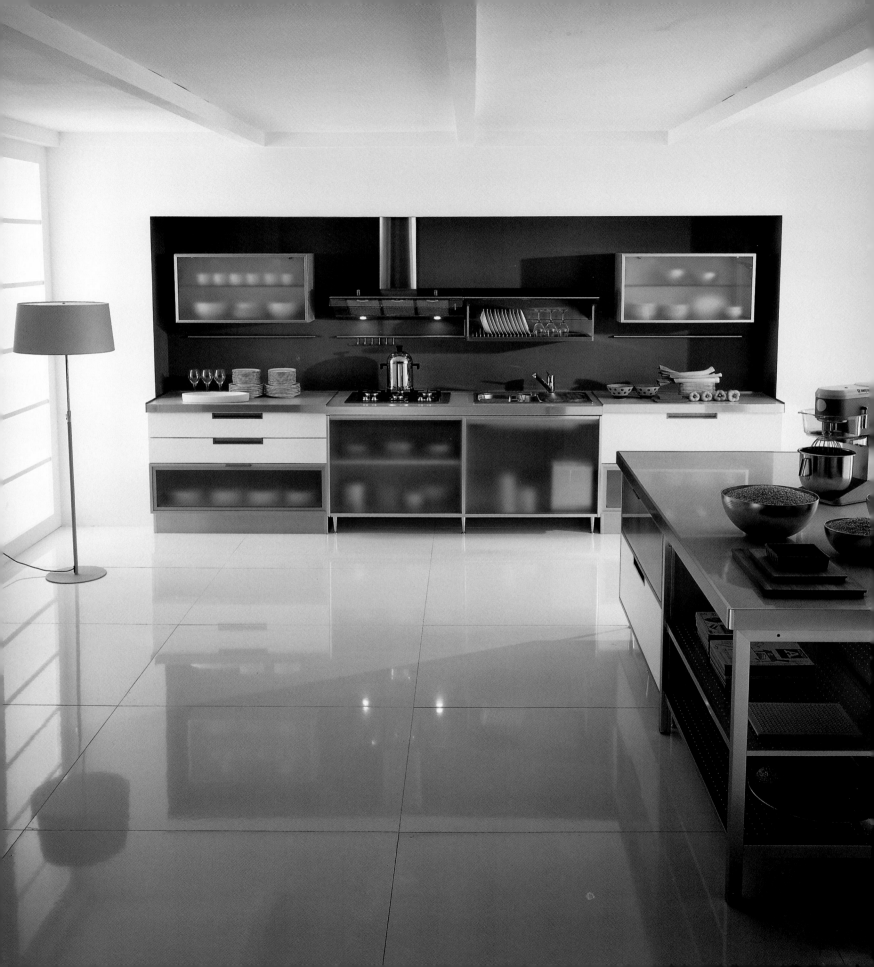

Color plays an essential role in creating more "human" environments that respond to the need to live surrounded by color. The direct and unmistakable perceptions brought to us by the brushstrokes of color, contrast with minimalism's particular lightness of shapes and forms, which at times appear to be diluted in space. When minimalism and color are united appropriately, and in just the right doses, the results are compositions that transmit harmony derived from the order of the parts. In these interiors, it looks like if nothing could be added or removed, because everything fulfils a determined function. The position and proportion of the different objects, of the empty spaces between them, and the distribution of color appear interrelated and form a compact whole. The distribution of these objects and colors must achieve a dynamic composition that transmits some tension when viewed, in order to avoid the monotony or boredom caused by a too neutral interior. The shapes, colors, textures and the light are resources that are capable of awakening centers of attention that, based on a certain asymmetry, generate movement.

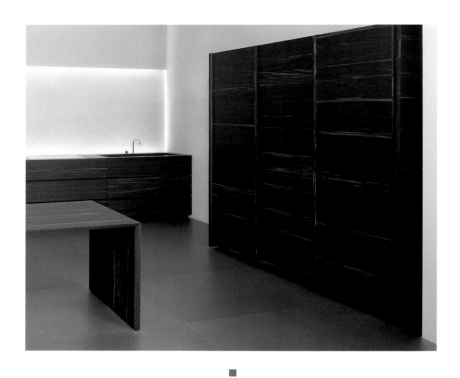

■

"I think it's difficult to design a
'beautiful table': it depends not only on
the instruments used, but also on a
subtle, fragile uncertain wisdom.
A wisdom with which, at some point in
time, someone, who knows how and who
knows why, manages to channel in the
project of an event the total perception
of our cosmic adventure, even though it
might be provisional, suspended and
incomprehensible."

Ettore Sottsass

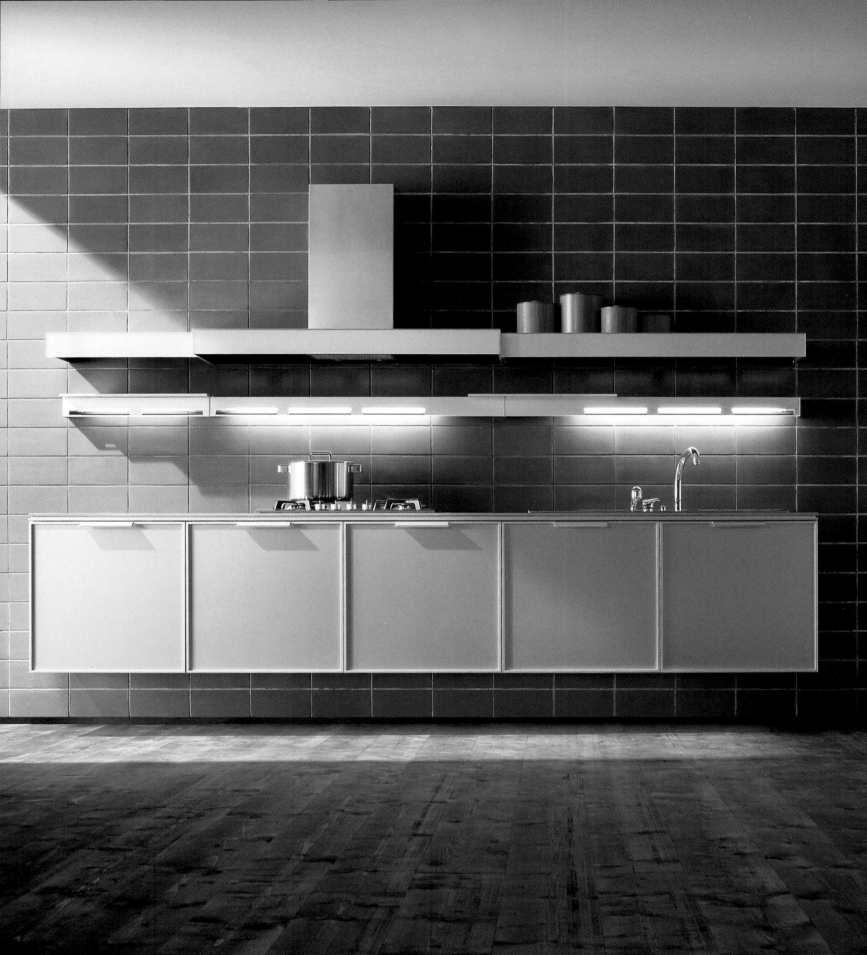

Minimalism implies an effort of reduction, which leaves in view only the indispensable, only the essence. Everything else is superfluous. And within this search for pure and naked geometric forms, color plays a predominant role because of its undisputed descriptive capacity, and the narrative discourse that it transmits in an implicit, unconscious, connotative way. The introduction of vibrant colors in a room, whether through furniture or painted walls, adds touches of visual impact that, in addition to bringing life to the atmosphere, break up the characteristic neutrality of the minimalist style. Even Zen defends the introduction of color in interiors, because of its concentrated individuality and its specific attributes, like the properties that a spice can add to a dish.

In an ambience characterized by emphasis on the fluidity of light and space, the subtleties of color take on special importance, showing the infinite effects produced by the variations of the textures. The effects that have the greatest impact are obtained by visually opposing textures and colors. By adding unexpected touches of brilliant or natural colors, the atmosphere is filled with new centers of attention, which personalize the aesthetic purity of the space. This is part of the evolution from the severest form of minimalism, correcting the error that is often made of identifying minimalism exclusively with the color white, a similar mistake to considering emptiness to be a lack of content.

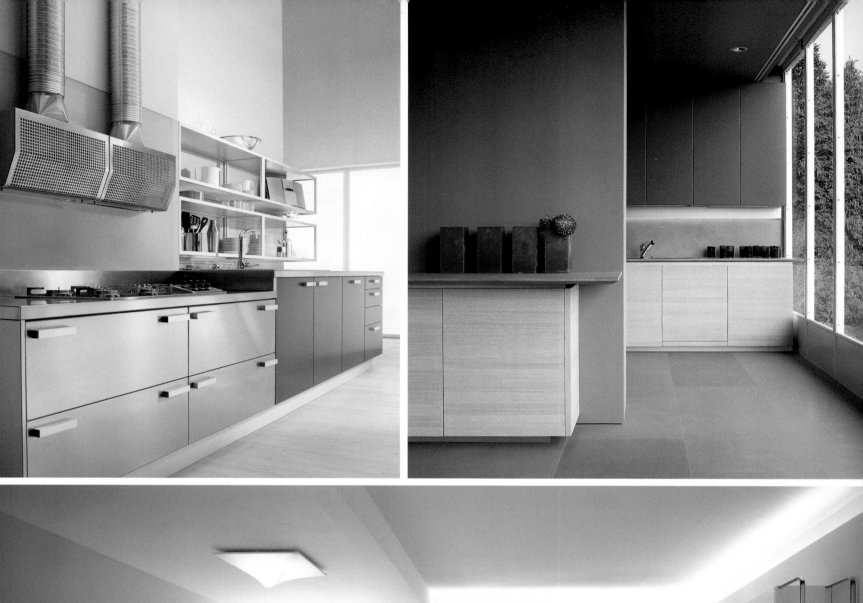
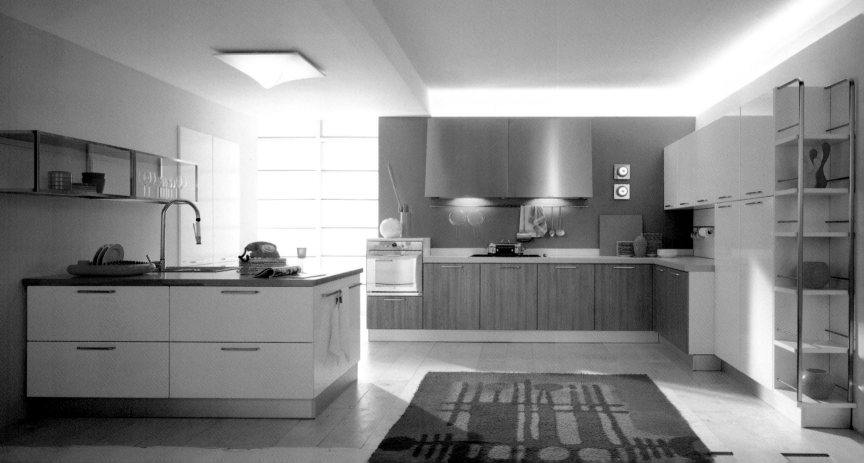

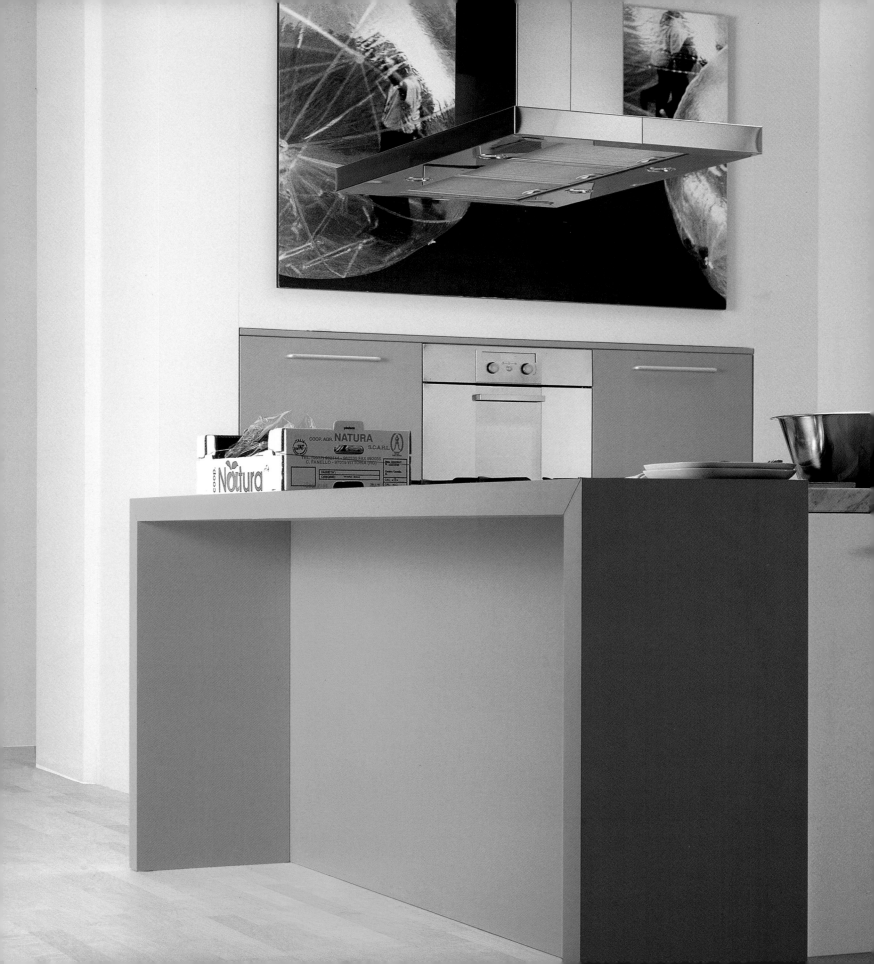

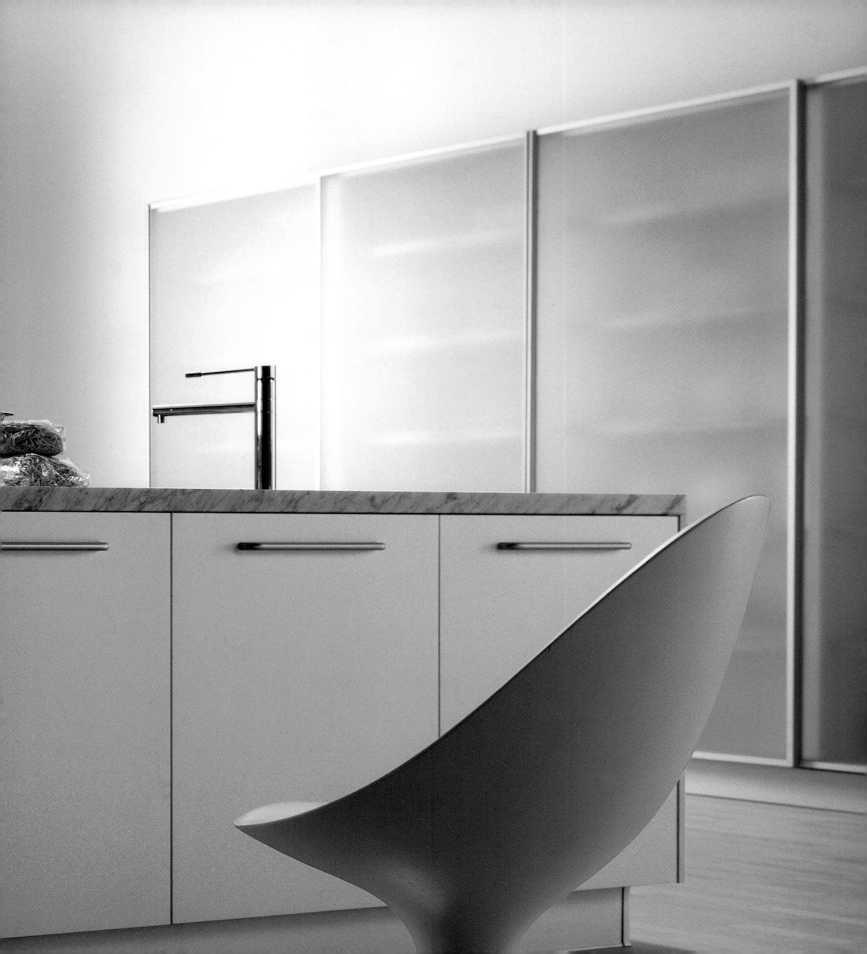

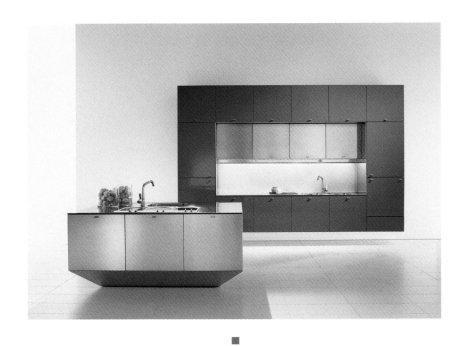

The warm colors par excellence are
yellow, orange and red. The latter is the
most intense, activating adrenaline more
than any other pure color and
establishing a suitable ambience
for conversation.

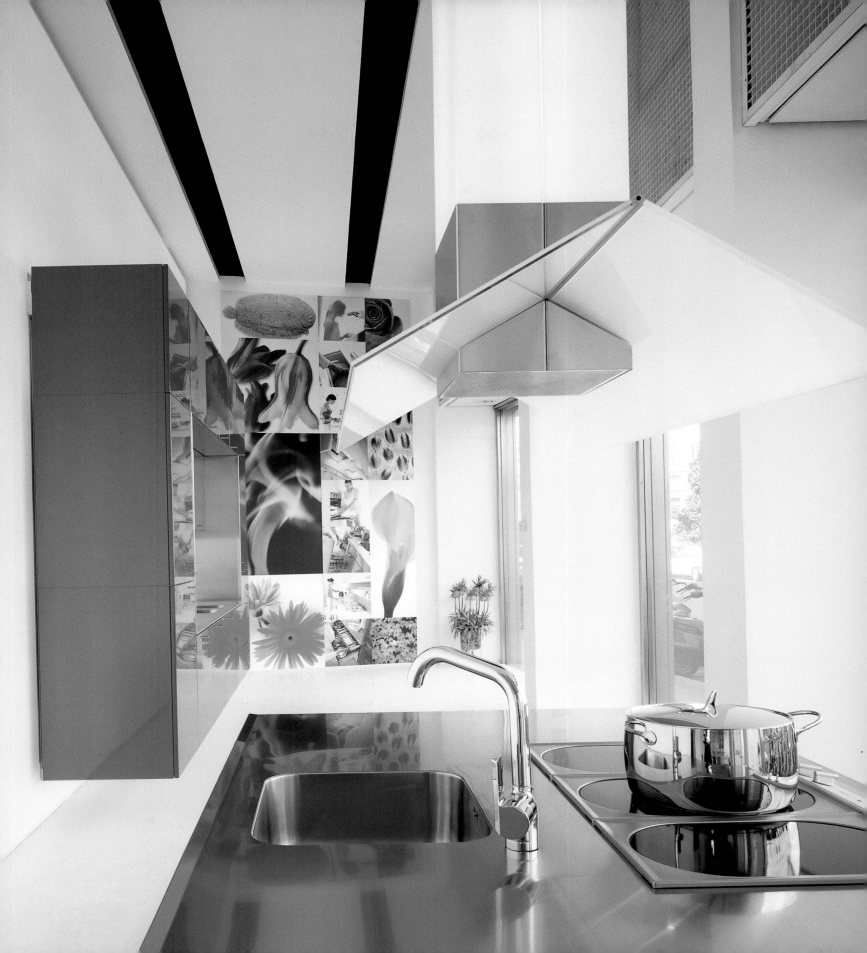

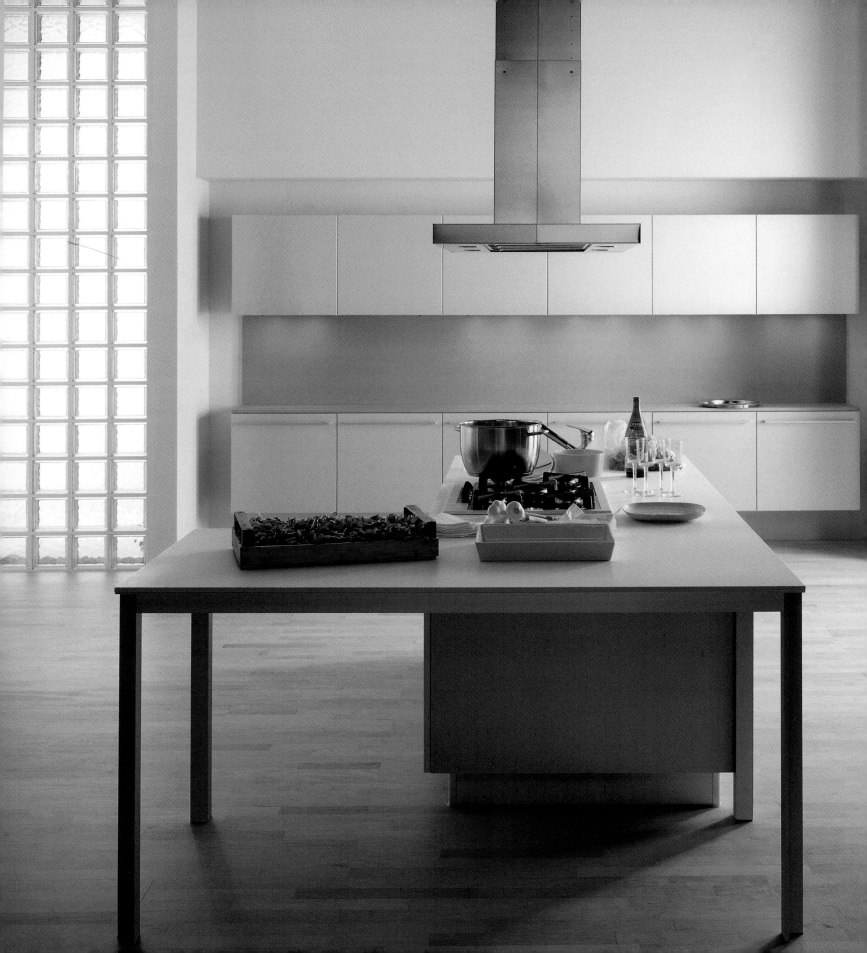

The space, the materials and textures and the light and the colors, become the fundamental pieces that give significance to these interiors. The choice of color is not at all fortuitous, because when so much depends on so little, each decision takes on a crucial importance. The different perspectives that we experience as we move around these environments, allow us to appreciate the delicate harmony of the whole, in which the colors contribute different sensations according to their lighting and their relationship with the other elements of the room. In this way, the emptiness is filled with content, establishing a balanced co-existence between simplification and the eloquence of color, which enriches the sensory experience.

In these interiors, the "less is more" of Mies van der Rohe leads to ambiences which find their fulfillment in geometric simplicity, austerity of emptiness, the emotive capacity of color and the dynamic force of the present. They replace the ornamentation of domestic space with a quest for maximum control over space. This has two direct consequences: on the one hand, the possibility of drawing a direct connecting line between architecture and interior decorating; on the other hand, the necessity to be honest with oneself by means of a not only aesthetic but moral conviction, given that the elimination of the distractions in traditional houses, lays bare the imperfections, not only of the architecture, but also of the soul.

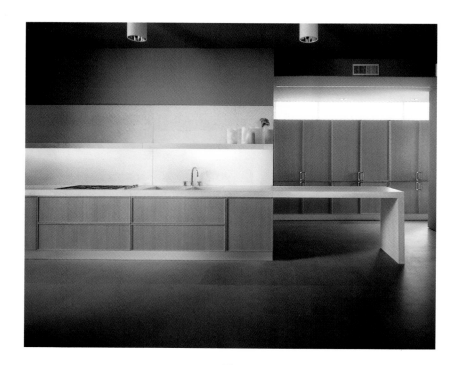

"The constant search for the archetypal
simplicity should justify, by itself, the
birth of a new object in our already
over-populated consumer society, without
adding gratuitous formal glitz introduced
in the project only to please the public."

Alberto Alessi

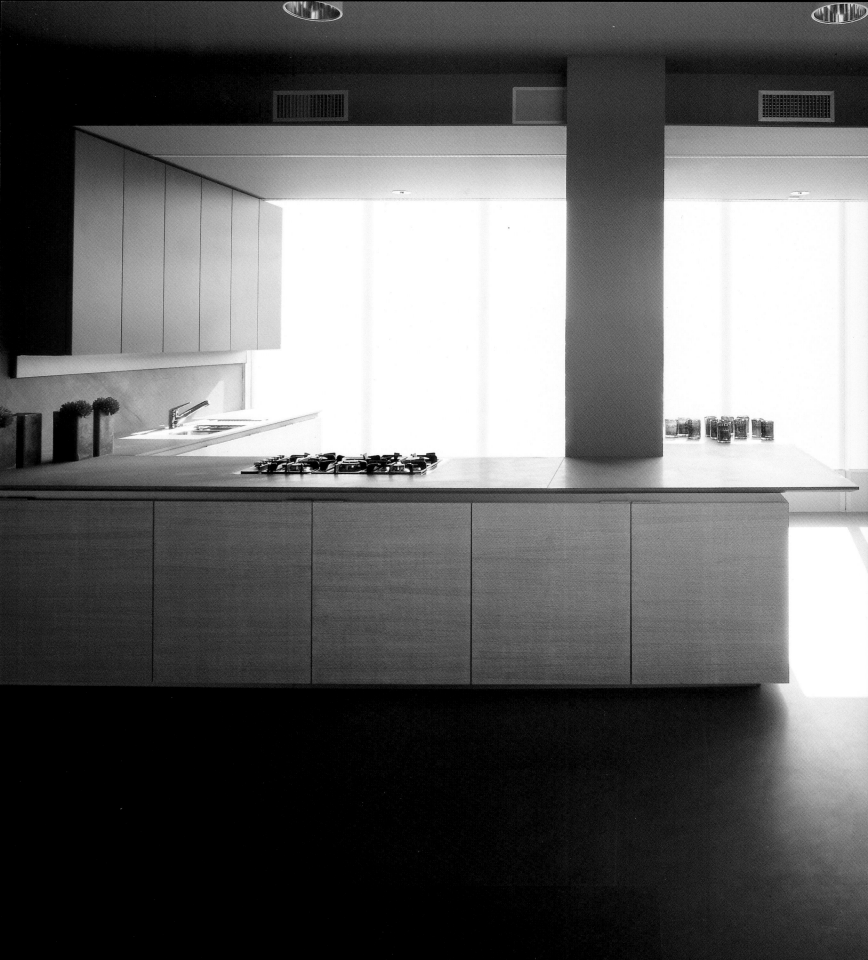

As an exercise in the simplification of the vital environment, minimalism is effort of introspection, which helps us to determine what is really important. Applied to our society, this does not imply reaching the extreme of the total austerity of a Shaker community or a Zen monastery, but each person must find the level of materialist reduction with which they feel comfortable. The main requirement is respect for space and for the subtleties of materials and details, learning to find beauty in the simplest of things. The fluidity of light through space, with its infinite play of light and shade, or the enormous impact that a color exercises over the general appearance of a room, are some of the subtleties laid bare by minimalist interiors.

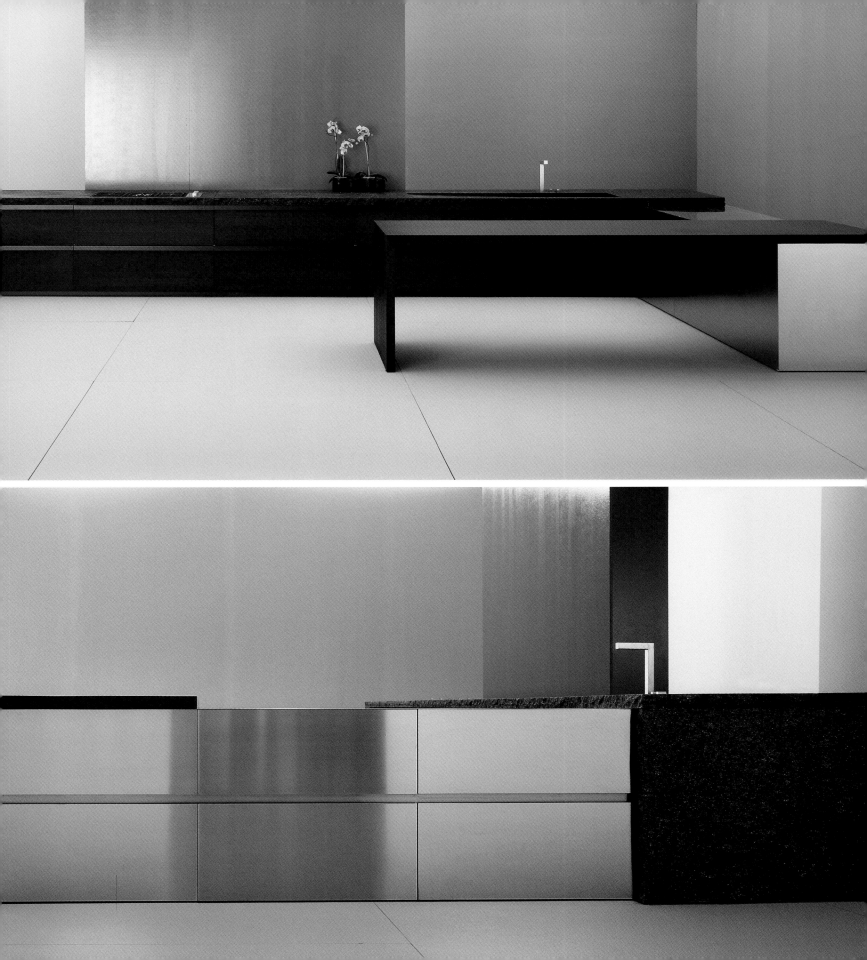

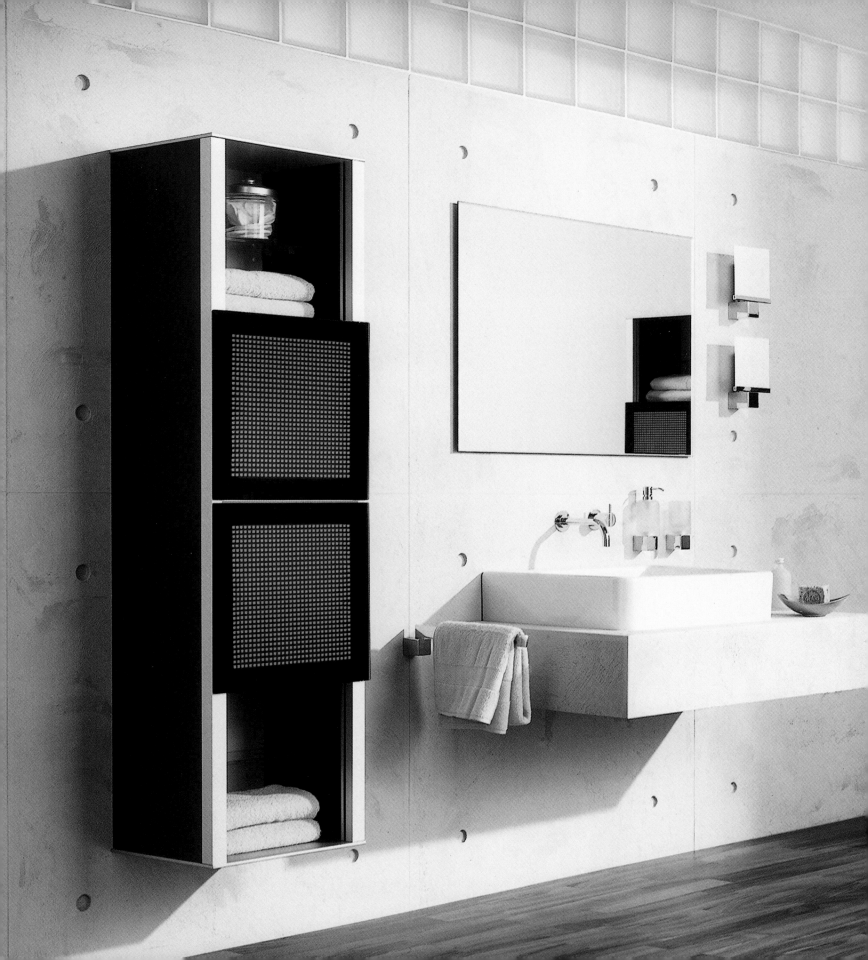

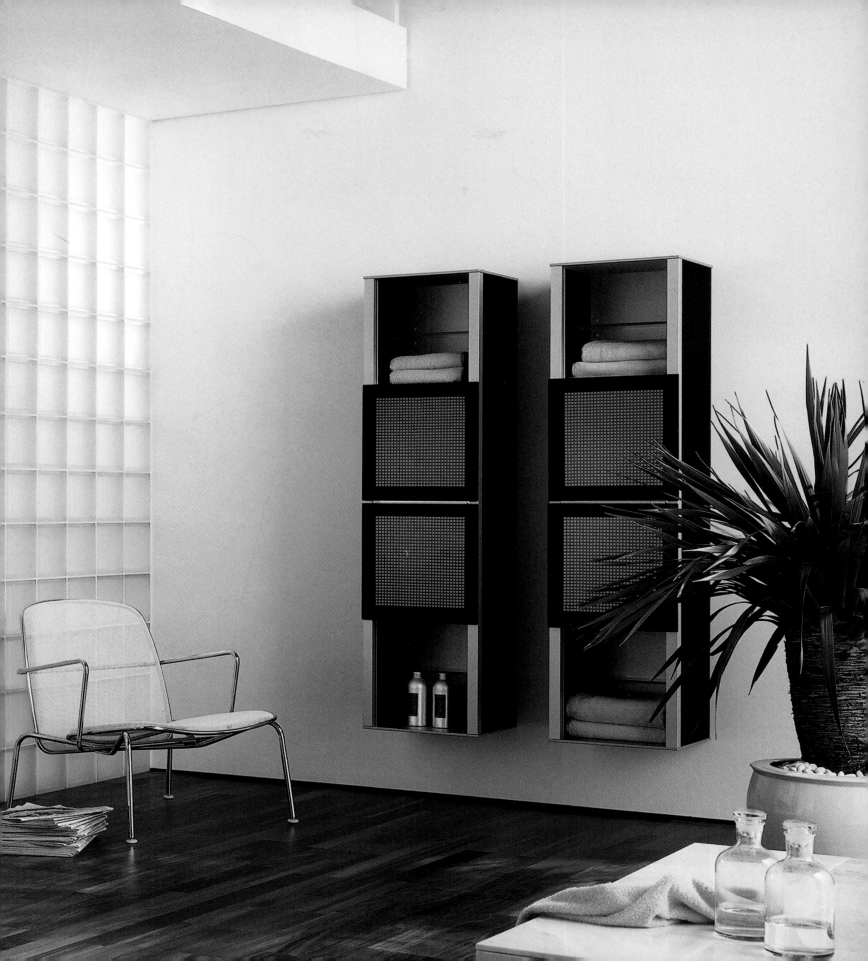

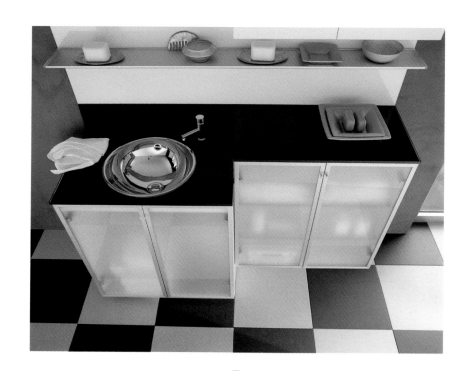

"The designer's function should be that
of someone who observes how people live
and who can visualize the way in which
things can be improved."

Niels Diffrient

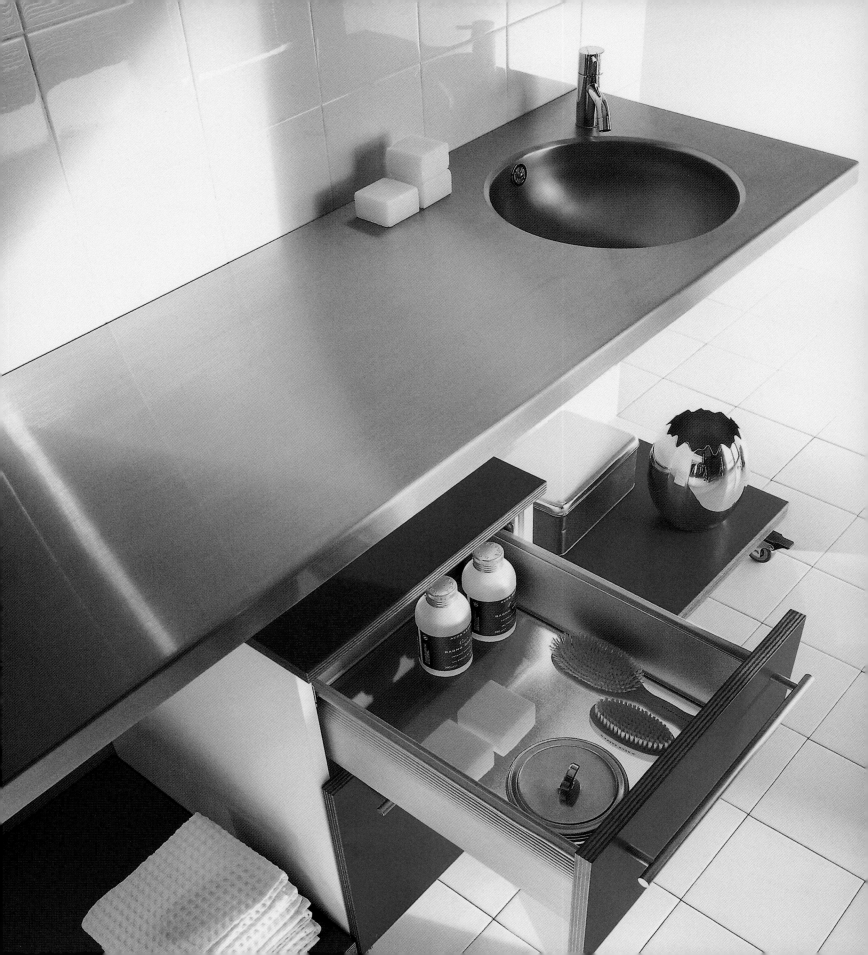

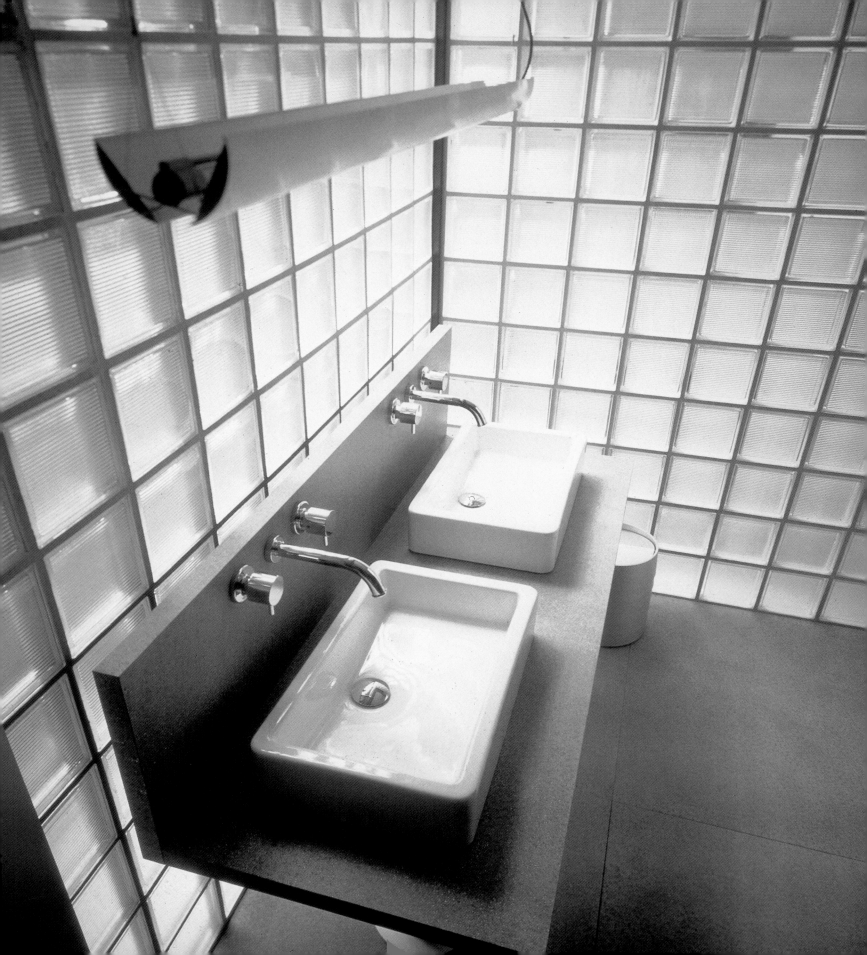

In an environment where visual, spatial and tactile sensations are central, and where every small detail is of essential importance, the effects that colors generate are basic to the achievement of a harmonious atmosphere. From the point of view of visual experience, harmony is understood as that which is pleasing to the eye. Consequently, in an ambience where chromatic harmony reigns, an intrinsic sense of order and balance is created in the visual perception. When harmony is broken, the resulting whole transmits either chaos or boredom, depending on whether the stimulation is too high or too weak. There are a multitude of possible chromatic schemes or combinations that generate changes in the dynamic balance of interiors. For example, a color scheme based on the combination of complementary colors, like red and green, creates the maximum contrast and the maximum visual stability. Furthermore, if colors are applied correctly, sometimes audaciously, certain compositions can be obtained to achieve specific objectives, like, for example, to add depth to a room (like a white surface on a black wall), multiply the luminosity with intense touches of yellow, or, on the contrary, to create shadowed areas, by the use of the color black, which absorbs light.

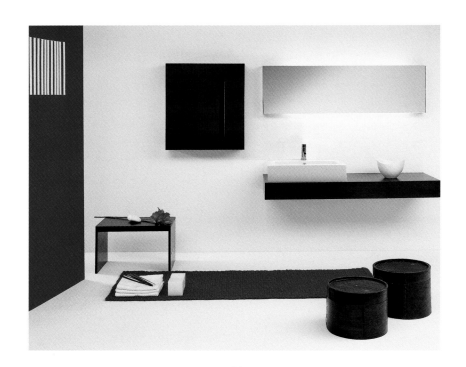

"It seems justified to affirm: the more
cultivated a people becomes, the more
decoration disappears."

Le Corbusier, 1925

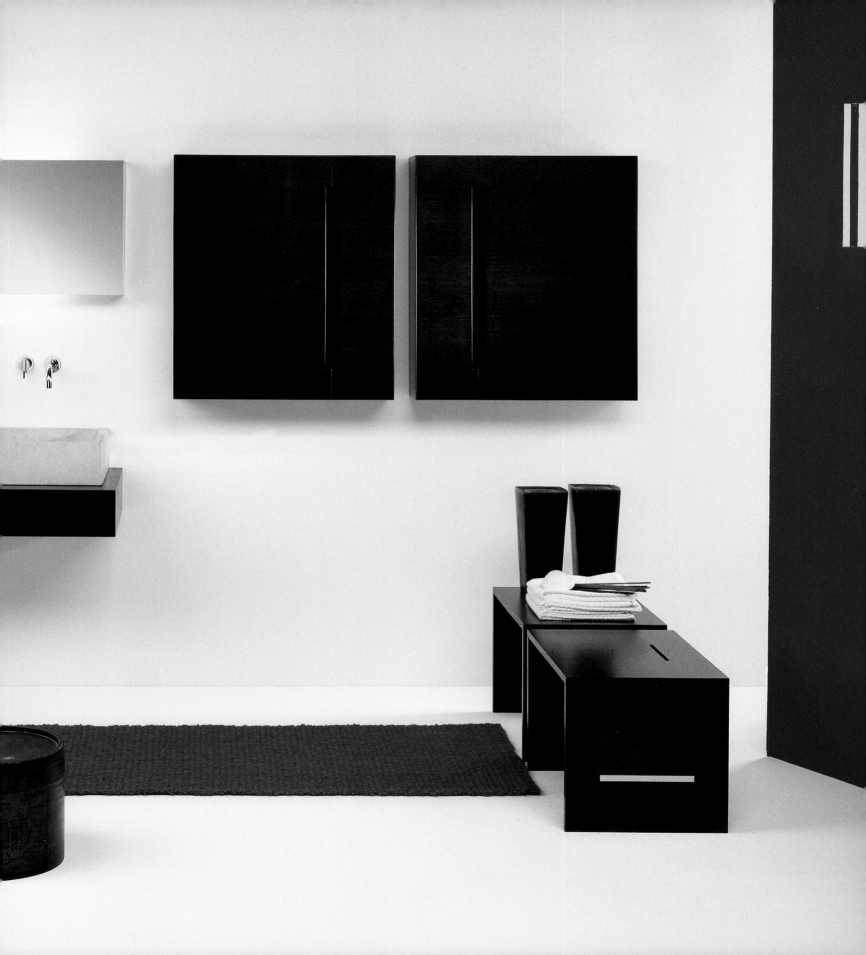

In conclusion, we can state that the evolution of minimalism is supported by strong contrasts between the neutrality of light colors and the introduction of intense accents of color. Also in this sense, it is necessary to exercize restraint and precision, which preserves the empty space. The combination of minimalism and color should allow the final result to remain faithful to the minimalist principle of formal reduction, strengthening the capacity to get rid of everything that is not essential. Functionalism and simplicity should be the starting point when choosing furniture, textures and colors, taking into account how they are inter-related. Thus the postulates of the strictest minimalism, whose extreme perfection and austerity gave rise on numerous occasions to houses more like an abode for the gods than habitable space for mere mortals are humanized.

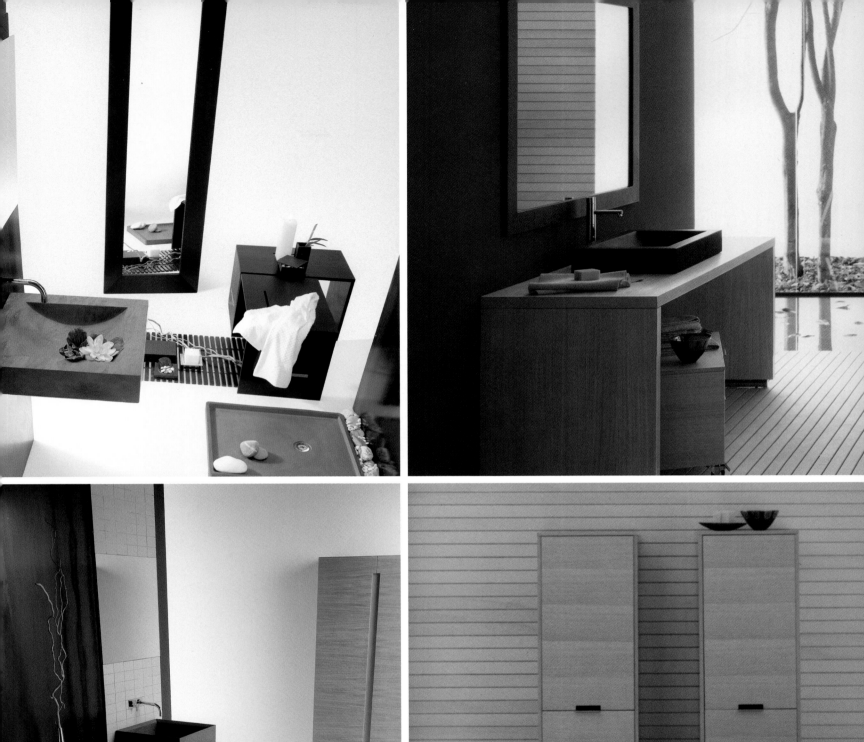
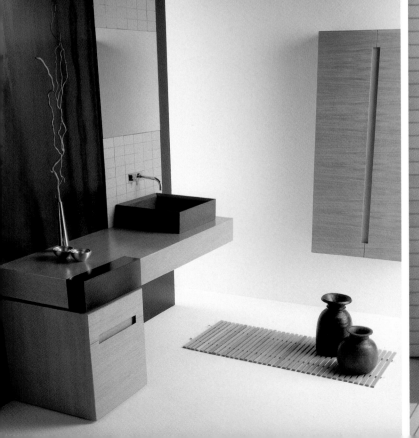
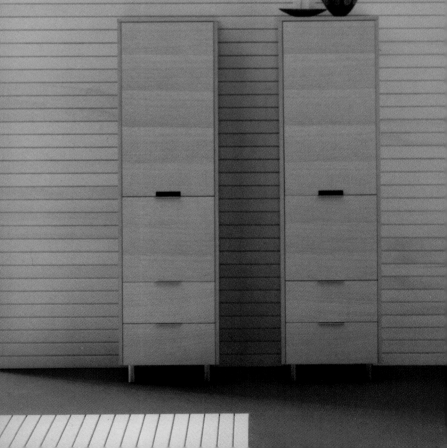

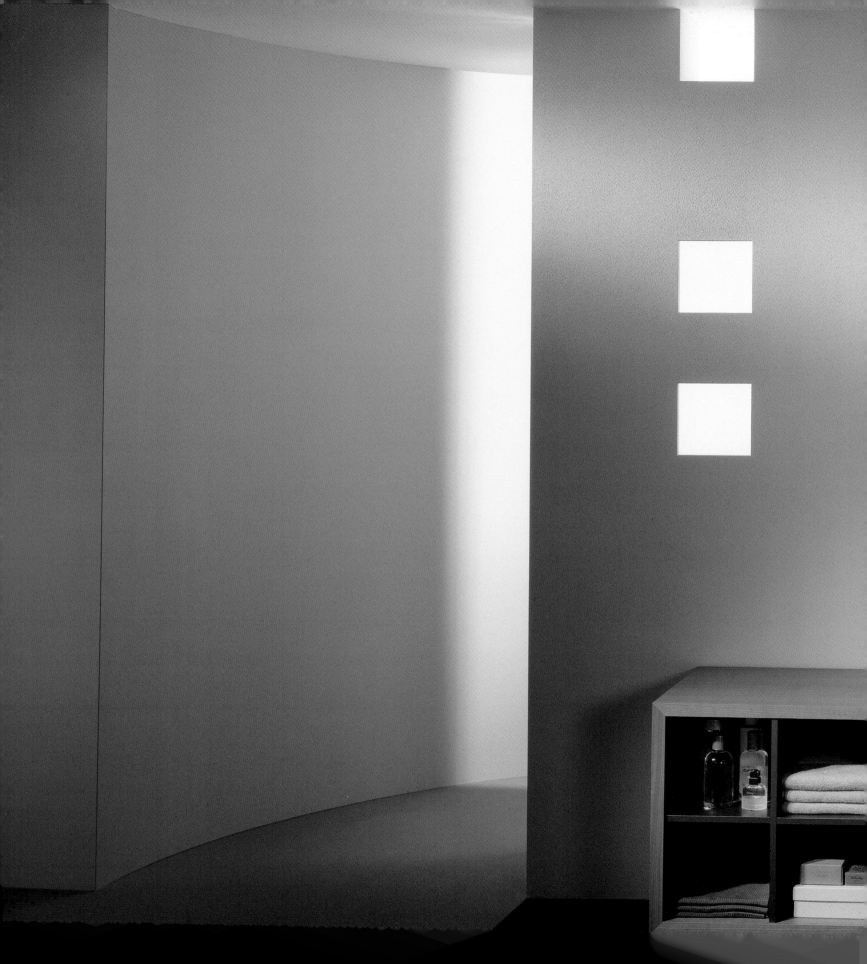

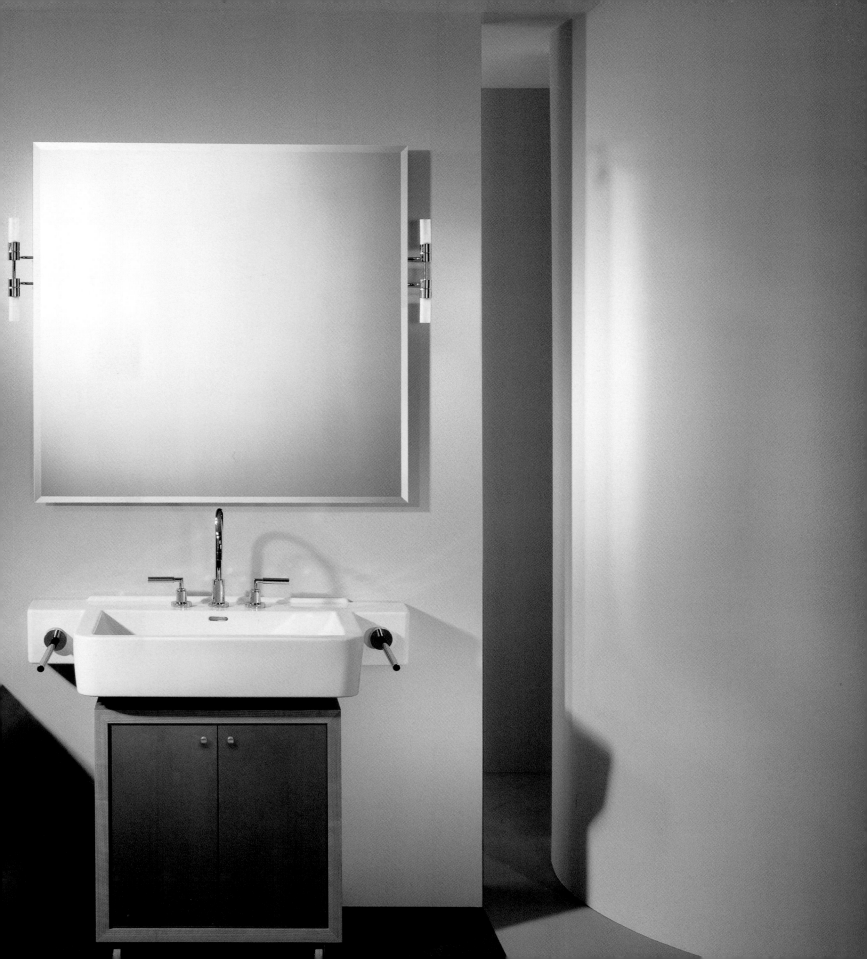

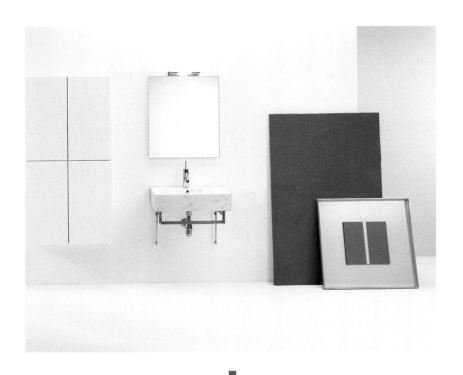

The concentration of mental energies
in the subtleties of proportion are
located at the very heart of the
minimalist mystery.

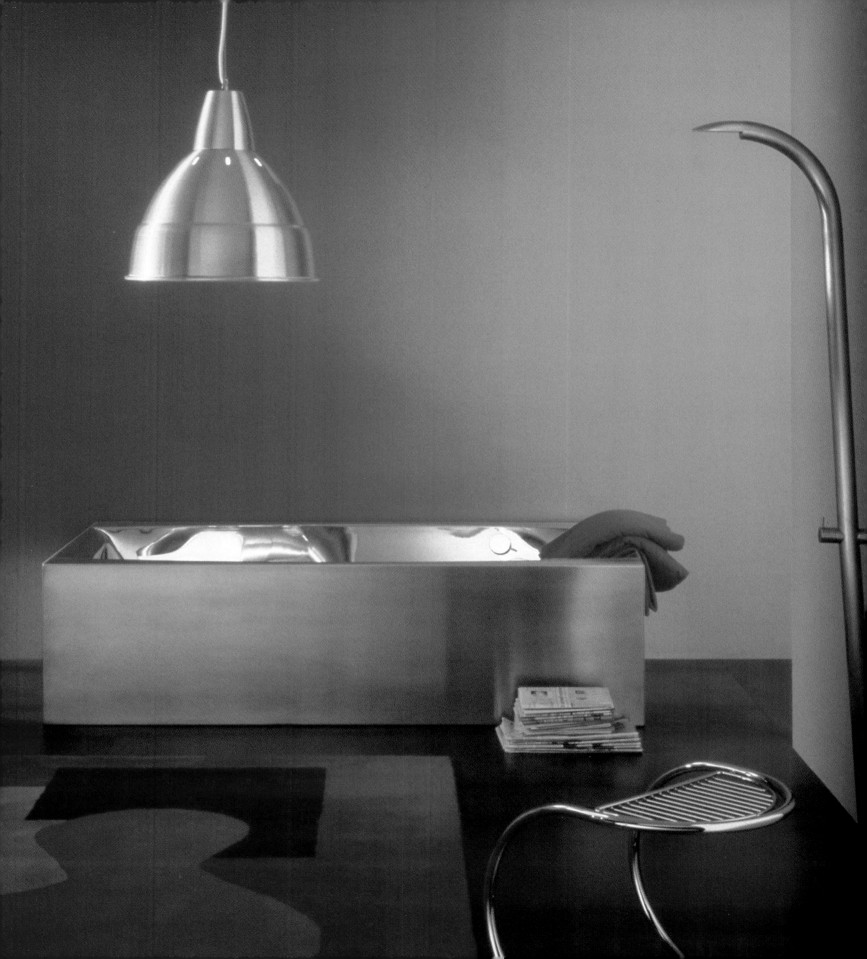

Minimalist interiors are therefore allied with the power of color, becoming friendlier and more flexible. From the premise of eliminating disorder, confusion and the superfluous, as a way to recuperate form and a sense of our environment, interiors are reduced to the basic, becoming a universal style that everyone can enjoy. By showing the elements in the simplest and clearest way possible, an environment is created which appeals directly to the senses. As a philosophy aiming to improve society, minimalism establishes the guidelines to eliminate distractions and material things from the domestic environment, creating homes where people can find balance. This effort of simplification creates spaces with a wider margin of freedom, where the individual feels like the master of the habitable space, not like its servant.

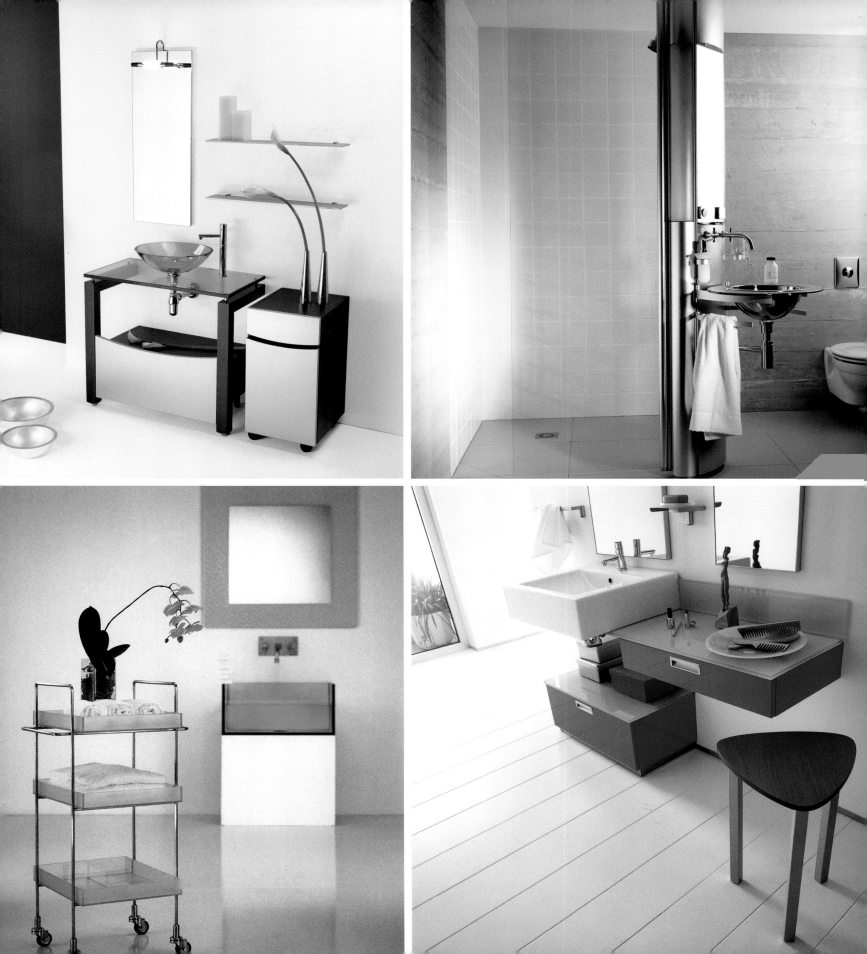

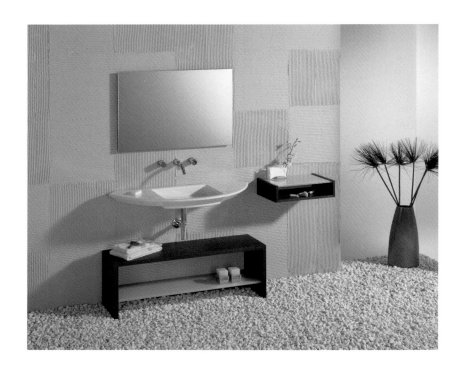

"Whether people are conscious or not,
they currently obtain their countenance
and their sustenance from the
atmosphere of the things they live with.
They are rooted in them, just like the
plant is rooted in the earth."

Frank Lloyd Wright

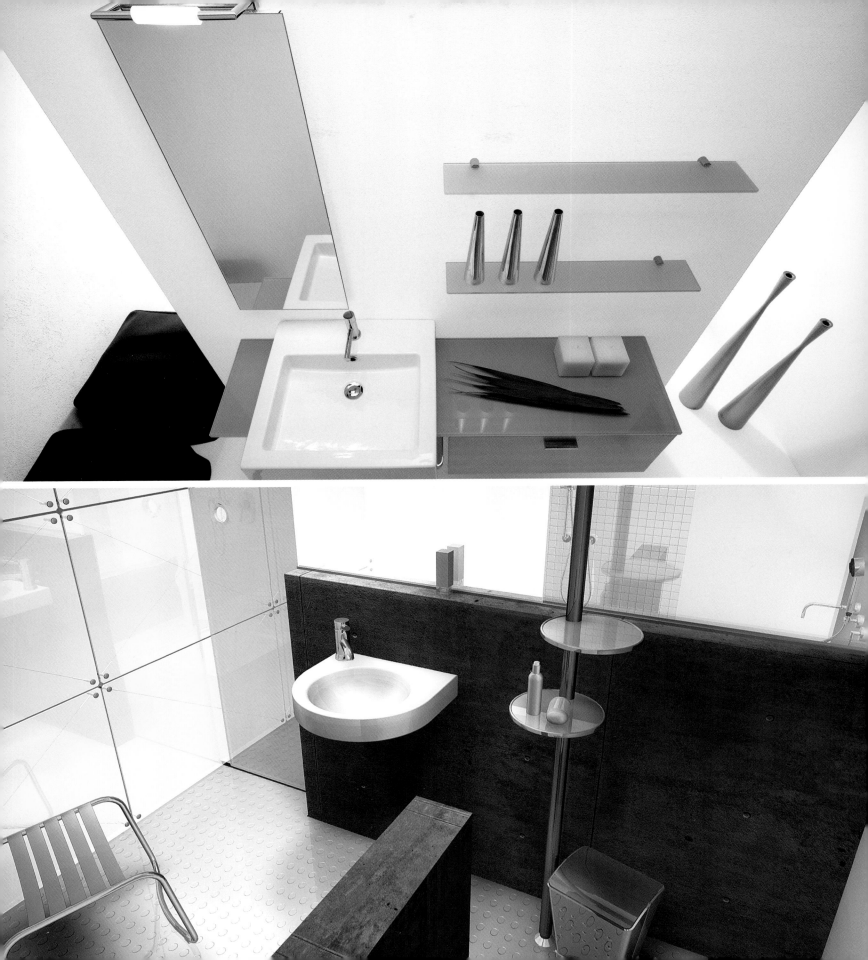

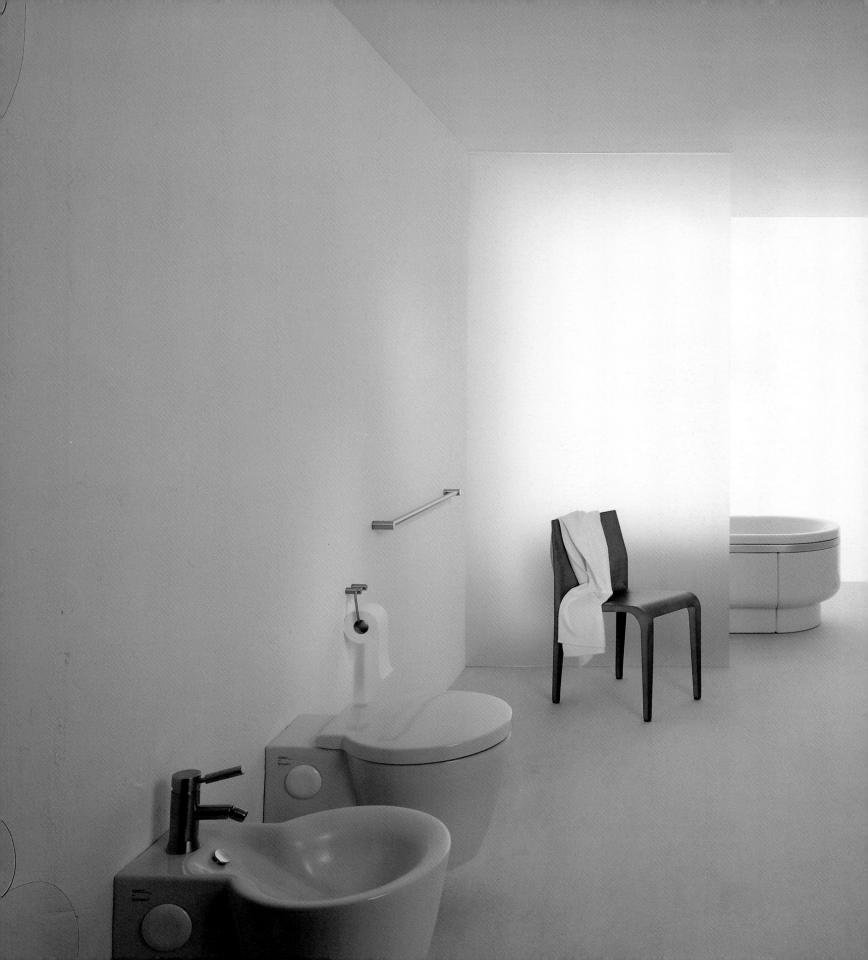

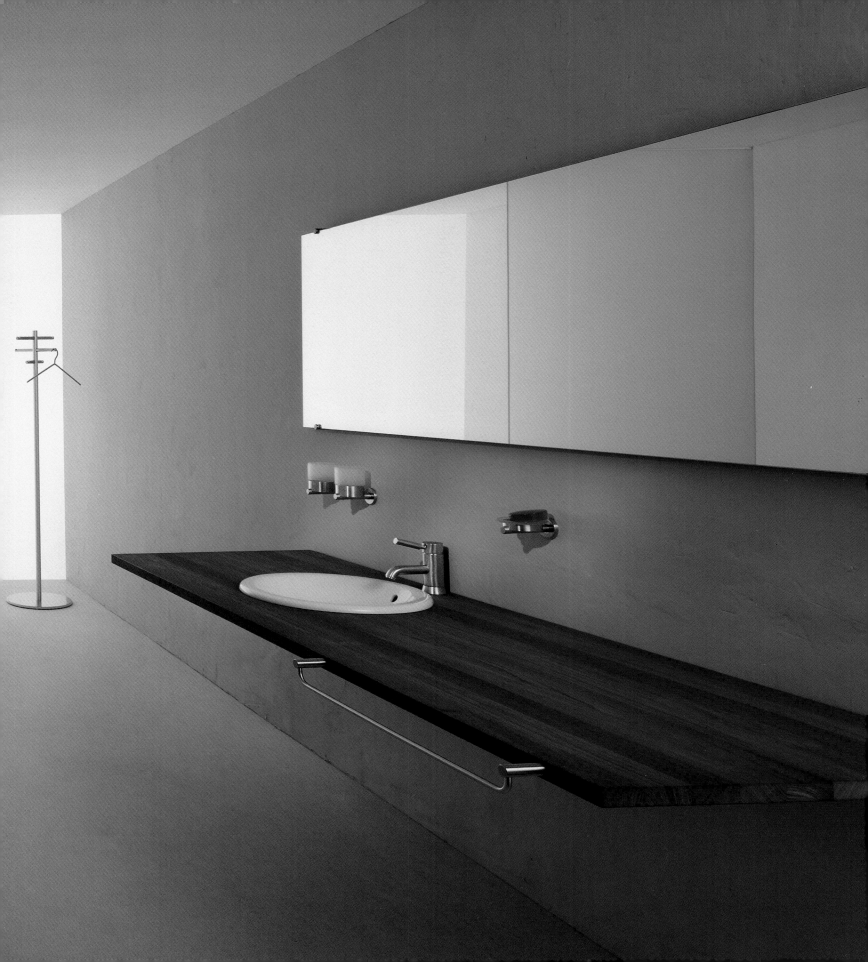

Image index

directory

ACERBIS International spa
Via Brusaporto 31
24068 Seriate (Bg)
ITALIA
Tel. + 39 035 294 222
Fax.+ 39 035 291 454
info@acerbisinternational.com

ALNO AG
88629 Pfullendorf
ALEMANIA
Tel. + 49 (0) 7552 21-0
Fax. + 49 (0) 7552 213 789
mail@alno.de

ARTQUITECT
C/Comercio, 31
08003 Barcelona
ESPAÑA
Tel. + 34 932 683 096
Fax.+ 34 932 687 773
artquitect@artquitect.net

AXIA srl
Via delle Querce 9
31033 Castelfranco Veneto (Treviso)
ITALIA
Tel. + 39 0423 496 222
Fax.+ 39 0423 743 733
axia@axiabath.it

B&B ITALIA spa
Strada Provinciale 32
22060 Novedrate (Como)
ITALIA
Tel. + 39 031 795 213
Fax.+ 39 031 795 224
beb@bebitalia.it

BELLATO
Via Azzi, 36
31040 Castagnole di Paese (Tv)
ITALIA
Tel. + 39 0422 438 800
Fax.+ 39 0422 438 555
infobellato@pallucobellato.it

BIS BIS IMPORTS BOSTON
4 Park Plaza
2116 Boston
ESTADOS UNIDOS
Tel. + 1 617 350 7565
Fax.+ 1 617 482 2339
info@bisbis.com

CALLIGARIS
Viale Trieste, 12
33044 Manzano (Udine)
ITALIA
Tel. + 39 0432 748 211
Fax.+ 39 043 250 104
info@calligaris.it

CATTELAN ITALIA spa
Via Pilastri 15 z.i. Ovest
36010 Carre' (Vi)
ITALIA
Tel. + 39 0445 318 711
Fax.+ 39 0445 314 289
info@cattelanitalia.com

CLUB 8 COMPANY
Fabriksvej, 4 -P.O. Box 74
6870 Ogold
DINAMARCA
Tel. + 45 7013 1366
Fax.+ 45 7013 1367
club8@club8.com

COR SITZMÖBEL
Nonenstraße 12
D-33378 Rheda-Wiedenbrück
ALEMANIA
Tel. + 49 (0) 5242 4102-0
info@cor.de

DAB (DISEÑO ACTUAL BARCELONA)
Avda. de la Cerdanya, Nau 10;
Pol. Ind. Pomar de Dalt
8915Badalona (Barcelona)
ESPAÑA
Tel. + 34 934 650 818
Fax.+ 34 934 654 635
info@dab.es

DADA
Strada Provinciale 31
20010 Mesero
ITALIA
Tel. + 39 029 720 791
Fax.+ 39 0297 289 561
dada@dadaweb.it

DO+CE MUEBLES DOCE,S.L.
Pol.Ind.Massanassa C/N.1 Nave 44
46470 Massanassa (Valencia)
ESPAÑA
Tel. + 34 961 252 467
Fax.+ 34 961 252 554
doce@do-ce.com

DORNBRACHT
Köbbingser Mühle, 6
58640 Iserlohn
ALEMANIA
Tel. + 49 (0) 2371 433 0
Fax.+ 49 (0) 2371 433 232
mail@dornbracht.de

DURAVIT ESPAÑA
Balmes 184, 4° 1ª
08006 Barcelona
ESPAÑA
Tel. + 34 932 386 020
Fax.+ 34 932 386 023
info@es.duravit.com

E15 GMBH
Hospitalstraße 4
61440 Oberursel
ALEMANIA
Tel. + 49 (0) 6171 582 577
Fax.+ 49 0 61 71 582 578
asche@e15.com

ELLEDUE ARREDOBAGNO - GRUPO COPAT
Viale L. Zanussi, 9
33070 Maron di Brugnera (Pn)
ITALIA
Tel. + 39 0434 617 111
Fax.+ 39 0434 617 212
info@copat.it

FEBAL CUCINE
Via Provinciale 11
61025 Montelabbate
ITALIA
Tel. + 39 0721 426 262
Fax.+ 39 0721 426 284
export@febal.it

GIORGETTI spa
Via Manzoni 20
20036 Meda (Mi)
ITALIA
Tel. + 39 036 275 275
Fax.+ 39 036 275 575
giorspa@giorgetti-spa.it

GLAS
Via Cavour 29
20050 Macherio (Mi)
ITALIA
Tel. + 39 0392 323 202
Fax.+ 39 0392 323 212
glas@glasitalia.com

HORM
Via Crocera di Corva, 25
33082 Azzano Decimo (Pordenone)
ITALIA
Tel. + 39 0434 640 733
Fax.+ 39 0434 640 735
horm@horm.it

HOUSE SISTEMA-GRUPO COPAT
Viale L. Zanussi, 9
33070 Maron di Brugnera (Pn)
ITALIA
Tel. + 39 0434 617 111
Fax.+ 39 0434 617 212
info@copat.it

INGO MAURER GmbH
Kaiserstrasse 47
80801 München
ALEMANIA
Tel. + 49 (0) 89381 6060
Fax.+ 49 (0) 89381 60620
www.ingo-maurer.com

JUVENTA
Slipstraat, 4
8880 Ledegem
BÉLGICA
Tel. + 32 56 50 01 91
Fax.+ 32 56 50 39 37
juventa@juventa.be

KERAMAG AG
Kreuzerkamp 11
D-40878 Ratingen
ALEMANIA
Tel. + 49 (0) 2102/916-0
Fax.+ 49 (0) 2102/916-245
info@keramag.de

KEUCO GmbH
Postfach 1365
D-58653 Hemer
ALEMANIA
Tel. + 49 (0) 2372 90 4-0
Fax.+ 49 2372 90 42 36
info@keuco.de

KLENK COLLECTION
Industriestraße 34
72221Haiterbach
ALEMANIA
Tel. + 49 (0) 7456 938 20
Fax.+ 49 (0) 7456 93 82 40
klenk-collection@t-online.de

LAGO srl
Via Morosini 22/24
35010 San Giogio in Bosco (Padova)
ITALIA
Tel. + 39 0495 994 299
Fax.+ 39 0495 994 199
info@lago.it

LUBE OVER CUCINE
Dell'Industria 4
62010 Treia
ITALIA
Tel. + 39 07 338 401
Fax.+ 39 0733 840 115
www.lubeover.it

MAISA sas
Corso Garibaldi 80
20020 Seveso (Mi)
ITALIA
Tel. + 39 0362 500 971
Fax.+ 39 0362 500 974

MATTEO GRASSI
Via Padre Rovanati, 2
22066 Mariano Comense
ITALIA
Tel. + 39 031 757 711
Fax.+ 39 031 748 388
info@matteograssi.it

MAXALTO
Strada Provinciale 32
22060 Novedrate (Como)
ITALIA
Tel. + 39 031 795 213
Fax.+ 39 031 795 224
beb@bebitalia.it

METHODO srl
Via Molinetto, 70
31030 Saletto di Breda di Piave (TV)
ITALIA
Tel. + 39 0422 686 132
Fax.+ 39 0422 686 587
info@methodotp.com

MINOTTI CUCINE
Via Napoleone, 31
37015 Ponton (Vr)
ITALIA
Tel. + 39 0456 860 464
Fax.+ 39 0457 732 678
info@minotticucine.it

MISURA EMME
Via IV Novembre, 72
22066 Mariano Comense(Co)
ITALIA
Tel. + 39 031 754 111
Fax.+ 39 031 754 111
info@misuraemme.it

SARILA (GRUPO MOBALPA) - Sté
Fournier
39 Rue de la Saulne, B.P. 22
74230 Thônes
FRANCIA
Tel. + 33 450 65 53 81
Fax.+ 33 450 65 52 04

MOBILEFFE spa
Via Ozanam, 4
20031 Cesano Maderno (Mi)
ITALIA
Tel. + 39 0362 502 212
info@mobileffe.com

mb - MOBLES BELLMUNT
C. del Puig, 12
08050 Roda de Ter (Barcelona)
ESPAÑA
Tel. + 34 938 500 038
Fax.+ 34 938 500 245
moblesbellmunt@infonegocio.com

MÖLLER DESIGN
Residenzstraße 16
32657 Lemgo
ALEMANIA
Tel. + 52 61 98 59-5
Fax.+ 52 61 8 92 18
info@moeller-design.de

NANI MARQUINA
Carrer Església 4-6, 3er D
08024 Barcelona
ESPAÑA
Tel. + 34 932 376 465
Fax.+ 34 932 175 774
info@nanimarquina.com

PERFORMA gmbh
Marbacher Straße 54
D-74385 Pleidelsheim
ALEMANIA
Tel. + 49 (0) 7144 898 869
Fax.+ 49 (0) 7144 898 876
tratsch@performa.de

PEROBELL
Avda. Arraona 23
08205 Sabadell (Barcelona)
ESPAÑA
Tel. + 34 937 457 900
Fax.+ 34 937 271 500
info@perobell.com

POGGENPOHL
Poggenppohlstraße 1
32051 Herford
ALEMANIA
Tel. + 49 (0) 5221 3 81
Fax.+ 49 (0) 5221 3 81 3 21
info@poggenpohl.de

POLIFORM spa
Via Monte Santo 28
22044 Inverigo (Como)
ITALIA
Tel. + 39 0316 951
Fax.+ 39 031 699 444
info.poliform@poliform.it

PORRO INDUSTRIA MOBILI srl
Via per Cantu' 35
22060 Montesolaro (Como)
ITALIA
Tel. + 39 031 780 237
Fax.+ 39 031 781 529
info@porro.com

RAPSEL
Via Volta 13
20019 Settimo Milanese (Milano)
ITALIA
Tel. + 39 023 355 981
www.rapsel.it

RATTAN WOOD spa
Via S.Rocco 37
31010 Moriago (Treviso)
ITALIA
Tel. + 39 0438 966 307
Fax.+ 39 0438 966 413
info@rattanwood.it

ROBOTS spa
Via Galvani 7
20082 Binasco (Milano)
ITALIA
Tel. + 39 029 054 661
Fax.+ 39 029 054 664
info@robots.it

ROCA
Avda. Diagonal, 513
08029 Barcelona
ESPAÑA
Tel. + 34 933 661 200
Fax.+ 34 934 194 501
www.roca.es

ROCHE BOBOIS
Muntaner, 266-268
08021 Barcelona
ESPAÑA
Tel. + 34 932 404 056
Fax.+ 34 934 140 873
www.rochebobois.fr

SANTA & COLE
Stma. Trinidad del Monte, 10
08017 Barcelona
ESPAÑA
Tel. + 34 934 183 396
Fax.+ 34 934 183 812
info@santacole.com

SCAVOLINI SPA
Via Risara 60-70/ 74-78
61025 Montelabbate
ITALIA
Tel. + 39 07 214 431
Fax.+ 39 0721 443 404
contact@scavolini.com

TECTA
Sohnreystraße 10
37697 Lauenförde
ALEMANIA
Tel. + 49 (0) 5273 378 90
Fax.+ 49 (0) 5273 378 933
info@tecta.de

TISETTANTA spa
Via Tofane, 37
20034 Giussano (Mi)
ITALIA
Tel. + 39 03 623 191
www.tisettanta.it

TOSCOQUATTRO srl
Via Sila, 40 c
59100 Prato
ITALIA
Tel. + 39 0574 815 535
Fax.+ 39 0574 815 384
toscoquattro@toscoquattro.it

TRIANGOLO S.R.L.
Via Icaro 10
61100 Pesaro
ITALIA
Tel. + 39 07 214 253
Fax.+ 39 0721 425 325
triangolo@triangolo.com

VERARDO spa
Via Porderone, 28
33070 Tamai (PN)
ITALIA
Tel. + 39 0434 600 311
Fax.+ 39 0434 627 155
valentina.b@verardoitalia.it

VICCARBE
Travesia Camí del racó, s/n
46469 Beniparrell (Valencia)
ESPAÑA
Tel. + 34 961 201 010
Fax.+ 34 961 211 211
viccarbe@viccarbe.com

VIELER INTERNATIONAL
Breslauer Straße 34
D-58614 Iserlohn
ALEMANIA
Tel. + 49 (0) 2374/52-0
Fax.+ 49 (0) 2374 52268
info@vieler.com

ZANETTE spa
Via Trieste 4
33070 Maron di Brugnera (Pordenone)
ITALIA
Tel. + 39 0434 623 151
Fax.+ 39 0434 624 298
info@zanette.it

ZANOTTA spa
Via Vittorio Veneto 57
20054 Nova Milanese (Mi)
ITALIA
Tel. + 39 03 624 981
Fax.+ 39 0362 451 038
zanottaspa@zanotta.it